GLOBAL CONTENT
QUEST

GLOBAL CONTENT
QUEST

In Search of
BETTER
TRANSLATIONS

IAN A. HENDERSON

For Françoise, who believed in the Quest
from the very beginning.

TABLE OF CONTENTS

INTRODUCTION

OPPORTUNITY

Hamburg, Germany, 1996

"Herzlich willkommen, Herr Henderson, Frau Henderson!"

Ian and Françoise were getting out of the car, when they heard Helga Berger call out to them.[1] She was standing in the doorway on the ground floor of the factory, sporting a big smile. "Welcome back to Germany," Helga said with a sly grin, "I think you will be surprised at how much has changed." Ian and Françoise looked at each other with curiosity. In the

---

1   All examples in this book are based on our experience. We have altered the names and locations, however, to protect the privacy of the individuals and companies involved.

years they had been visiting Helga at the AKIKO computer manufacturing plant in Hamburg, they had never seen her quite so animated. As the tech company's vice president of production, she always seemed to be furrowing her brow over a perplexing problem. Today she seemed almost jovial.

"Have you switched your product to magic wands?" Françoise joked.

"Some mornings it feels that way," said Helga with a wink.

On his way into the factory, Ian paused in the doorway. It was all he could do not to gasp out loud. It had been six months since he and Françoise had been there, and the transformation was astonishing.

Gone was the conveyer belt chugging along with a line of deconstructed products; gone was the droning sound of the mechanical assembly line and din of voices shouting to be heard; gone were the rows of workers, meticulously repeating their actions over and over again.

In place of this familiar sight was a completely new setup of six stations around a table. At each station sat a technician with a set of tools, working on a single computer and assembling the components. The work was quiet and fastidious but seemed light-years from the monotony and repetition of the previous configuration. Each worker was focused, determined, and relaxed—each helping to assemble the precious object by hand, from start to finish.

"That's remarkable," Ian said a few moments later, once they'd all sat down in Helga's sunny office down the hall. "I don't know if I've ever seen anything quite like it, not for a company this big."

"You probably haven't," Helga replied. "We've completely revamped our whole process, and I don't know if anyone else is doing it this way."

"And what is the process, exactly?"

"Rather than the conveyor belt, we've shortened the assembly line from fifty people to a group of six."

"And it is working?" Françoise asked.

Helga leaned in with a smile. "Beautifully. The build quality has gone way up, and we haven't lost any production time." Helga got up from her chair and wandered to the window that looked out onto the factory floor. Once full of loud, relentless, repetitive movement, it was now a calm and fluid atmosphere.

"I think it's because each technician is personally invested in each machine built," she said. "There is less compartmentalizing. Instead, they are thinking as a team about the computer as a whole from the first component to the last. They are thinking about it as a final product, in the hands of the user at the end of the journey."

Ian and Françoise looked at each other and smiled.

"What's the joke, you two?" Helga asked.

"Nothing! It's brilliant," said Françoise. "But you're wrong."

Helga sat back down with an incredulous smile. "I'm not wrong. Productivity and quality have both gone up, and it's because of a holistic approach."

"I have no doubt of that, Helga," said Ian. "You're wrong to say we've never seen it before. We've seen it before many times. Thinking about the whole product from the beginning of the journey—that's exactly how we approach translation."

OUR QUEST

My partner, Françoise, and I founded our translation company, Rubric, in 1994, because we were on a quest. We wanted to share our belief that *translation is not about linguistics; it is about content.*

Right now, you might be skeptical, thinking, "Really? But isn't translation simply the act of taking text from one language and translating it into another?"

If this were true it *would* be extremely simple.

But as anyone who has developed a product in the United States, and then tried to launch it in another country, will tell you: Approaching translation as merely a linguistic step in the process will lead to failure. This approach does not account for cultural specificity, local customs, platform discrepancies, or legal requirements. It is an approach that will also slow you down, cause endless frustration, and have a very negative impact on your budget.

The truth is, translation is so much more than translating words from one language to another. It is the act of communicating between cultures and continents. Translation is the key that can unlock the door to multiple spheres, and without it, your company cannot fully thrive internationally.

Still, many executives approach translation as though it is just a stop on the conveyor belt—usually the last. They think it can be a step tacked on at the end of the process—after the screws have been tightened, the packages have been sealed, and the copy has been written.

I am here to tell you this is wrong. Like the transformed factory floor at the AKIKO plant in Hamburg, translation is an integral part of the whole process, something that is best considered from the moment you begin to design your product. Translation is most effective when it is taken into consideration as part of the big picture, just like the team working together to build the computer from top to bottom.

This has always been our philosophy, and over the last few decades, we have developed long-lasting relationships with our clients because of the success of this notion. Over the years, we have encountered considerable obstacles, faced fascinating challenges, and collected a deep well of wisdom that has informed the way we do business. Everything along the way reinforced our belief that our holistic approach is the most effective path. Now we want to share this wisdom with you.

THE BILLION-DOLLAR MISTAKE

If you are like the many executives we work with in the United States, you are passionate and committed to your company and your product. It is a product or service that took years, possibly decades, to design, perfect, and disseminate into the world. As someone who has been in business for more than a quarter century, I understand what it means to care deeply about what you do. So here is an important question: Do you want to share what you do with the rest of the world?

The United States is big, but without tapping into the larger, global market, your revenue options are severely limited. After working so long and so hard to create a product or service that you know is of enormous value, it doesn't make sense to limit your customer base to people who happen to speak English. If customers have the opportunity to buy a product that "speaks to them" in their language, that's what they're going to do. Only 5 percent of people speak English as a first language, so, even if your product is smarter, sleeker, and sexier, you're going to miss out because you're not in conversation with the rest of the world.

One of the biggest concerns we hear from executives is the cost to translate. At the end of a long process, it may seem daunting to add another ten or twenty thousand dollars to the budget, especially if it comes as a surprise. However, what you must consider is the cost of *not* translating. Your attempt to save ten thousand dollars might end up being a billion-dollar mistake.

It's true that translation is not cheap. The more markets you want to conquer, the more languages you have to speak. However, once you begin to consider translation as an essential cost of doing business, not only will the investment seem minimal, but the whole endeavor will actually become less expensive. The earlier in the process you begin to account for multiple translations, the simpler, more effective, and less expensive the process becomes. Once a good translation process is in place, it won't be cost prohibitive—ultimately it will be far more *cost effective*.

Think of it this way: if you designed a toaster with an American plug, when it came time to sell it in Europe, you wouldn't say, "Just send it as it is and they'll figure it out." Likewise, you wouldn't watch the last toaster come off the assembly line, smack your head, and suddenly think, "Maybe we should make some with a European plug as well?"

Most likely, you would calculate European sales early in the process and integrate them into the overall plan. You would take the needs of the European market into consideration throughout the design and manufacturing process, because some very basic research would have alerted you to the fact that you would not sell any toasters in Europe without a European plug. The plug is easy to replace, but in Europe most countries run on 220V, unlike the US, where it is 110V. Easy to address early in the process, but harder later on.

Translation is the same. When we translate the user manuals, the print advertisements, the marketing emails, or anything else, we've been planning for this step from the very beginning. Even if you have not accounted for translation early in the process, it's not too late, and it is still important to get the right translation team with the right philosophy on board. A good team will maximize what assets you already have, ask you the right questions, and approach the project with thoroughness and passion. A good team will always be building knowledge for next time as well.

AKIKO WAS JUST THE BEGINNING

Just like the surprise that greeted us in Hamburg, our whole story of working with AKIKO has been exciting and unpredictable—and one from which we have all gleaned important lessons. Over the years working with them, we have been able to help them reach a billion-dollar market and become a leader in their industry.

One major example of our success with AKIKO is the cost of their manuals. Before we came on board with them, their translated user manuals cost eight thousand dollars per language, and had a production time of six weeks. In the nineties, when computers only had a shelf life of about three months, this was deadly for both the product and the bottom line. Over the course of our working relationship, we managed to drive the cost of that production down to seventy-five dollars a language and shrunk the turnaround time to just a few days. Eight thousand dollars to seventy-five dollars—six weeks to four days. It's almost like we took a long, cumbersome assembly line and turned it into a sleek, productive workstation.

There were many factors that allowed us to drive the manual costs for AKIKO down and help them increase their revenue. The most important thing to remember is that all of these steps were only possible because as a team, they bought in to our philosophy: translation is not merely about linguistics; it is about content and communication.

Throughout the course of this book we will talk about our quest, embarked on so many years ago, and how our clients like AKIKO have benefitted from it. We will also talk about how you can understand translation in a new way—a way that could transform your company and help you open up billions of dollars' worth of revenue on the international market.

1

MARSHY GROUND

PARIS, FRANCE, 1997

Ian held the paper in his hand and studied it, his stomach dropping. The fax had come through from California only moments before. He stared at it, trying to make sense of what he was seeing.

Sections were blurry, faint, and crooked. It looked as though the paper had been printed and copied multiple times before it came their way. Handwritten notes, some illegible, were scribbled in the margins. He looked down at the desk. Ten or so more pages like this one sat there. He closed his eyes with a deep sigh.

Françoise set down a cup of tea in front of him. He hadn't even heard her come in to the office.

"Is it that bad?" she asked with a smile.

"We're off in the wrong direction, that's for sure."

She sat down at the table with him, her self-possessed energy calming him. He picked up his cup and sipped the tea.

"Tell me: What's the problem?"

He held up the messy page at which he had been squinting. "I just got the fax. These are the documents we need to translate."

Her eyes widened. "Into what?"

"I think this is the first mailer," he said, pushing the page toward her. He reached for another page on the desk. "This one is the product license, and this one is the wording for the packaging."

"The packaging?" She sounded almost alarmed, taking the page from his hand. "How do we know what goes where? What part is for the consumer's eye, and what is the fine print?"

Ian leaned back in his chair with a chuckle. She looked at him and he shrugged. She considered the pages again.

"This is not their fault. No one ever explains to clients how translation really works," she said emphatically. "But it happens so often. If we don't explain it, how can we expect it to change?"

"I don't know if we can explain it."

"Nonsense," she said.

He smiled at her confidence. "Our whole job is communication. You're telling me we can't translate what we do into a language that engineers, lawyers, and marketing people can understand?"

Ian laughed. "You raise a good point."

Françoise put the paper down and sipped her own tea. Her eyes were in that far-off place that Ian recognized—the place where all her brilliant ideas came from.

"What are you thinking?"

"Well, we always talk about our journey to help people communicate with the world. The clients are on a journey, too, from the moment they start their product creation. But when they send us things like this, it is like they're setting off on the most important part of their journey, without a map of any kind. As though they are just wandering into the woods and expecting to find their way through without a plan to survive."

Ian was interested in this analogy. "Go on."

She leaned in, now excited about where this idea was taking her. "It's like when we worked with Dimensions last year on their product launch, and we had to redo all the work that their internal guy had done. What was his name?"

"Lorenzo."

"Right, Lorenzo. Such a nice guy, and helpful with product terminology, but his work as a translator wasn't good enough."

"I remember," said Ian, wincing a bit at the recollection.

"And with Destinations Worldwide last month. When we discovered that the information sheet we were working on had already been translated into Portuguese for the catalog, and no one had told us." She was animated by the idea now, tapping her leg as her mind worked.

"When we first started with AKIKO, and they had just spent all that money on translation software. They ended up having to scrap it after six months."

"Believe me, I know there are all kinds of problems companies run into when they embark on translation."

"But they don't see them; they can't foresee what they're facing. When they look out at the future, all they see is flat, straightforward terrain, despite that all kinds of things can go wrong."

"Yes, it's complicated."

"Well, in some ways it is, and in some ways it

isn't. You see, all the problems are different, yet the solution is quite simple."

Ian laughed. She always had some solution up her sleeve. "Do tell."

"They need to have a map. The only way to avoid these problems—these sink holes, soggy spots, and retreaded ground—is to know what you're dealing with from the outset and avoid them altogether."

She grabbed her cup again. "We have to help them develop a map for the journey. Otherwise, they're always going to end up on marshy ground."

> "We have to help them develop a map for the journey. Otherwise, they're always going to end up on marshy ground."

DRAWING THE MAP

Through our many years of translating, we have developed a philosophy and style that can help companies achieve enormous gains in efficiency, accuracy, and ultimately revenue. We are committed to giving our clients not only what they want, but also what they need—what will ultimately serve them best in the long term. Sometimes this means we have to push back on requests—ask more questions, inquire about different formats, deepen our understanding about intention and destination. In the end, all of our searching is in an effort to help our clients draw the map that Françoise identified as the key to success.

No matter what point we come on board with a company, we always have the larger picture in mind. Even if someone brings us in late to the process on a particular product, we immediately begin working on solutions and laying the groundwork for the future as well. Part of drawing a good map is collecting information from each outing. Lessons learned on our first excursion will surely come in handy on future journeys. Continued success is reliant on building long-term relationships with companies built on trust, competency, and institutional knowledge.

Every journey has the risk of pitfalls and perils, not unlike the ones described in the passage above. Long-term experience in the industry helps us know which problems to look for, and one-on-one working history with companies helps us design a precise and personalized plan to avoid them. On the whole, there are five specific, avoidable complications that tend to land people on marshy ground:

- Not understanding that the quality you put in will be the quality you will get out

- The "Lorenzo can do it" method

- Misapplied tools

- Being stuck in silos

- Poor user journeys

If you find yourself dealing with any (or in some cases, all) of these problems, it might mean you're out in the wilderness without a map. Do you find yourself dealing with constant crises, disasters, or setbacks? Does there always seem to be a fire to put out? Are you facing the same problems repeatedly, despite having been through them before? You're not alone, and it's not too late. Our quest to reorient the way you think about translation starts here, with these five complications that can land you on marshy ground.

YOU WILL GET OUT WHAT YOU PUT IN, FOR BETTER OR WORSE

The notion of "quality in, quality out" is well known to anyone in business, but there is often a disconnect between knowing the adage and understanding what counts as "quality." It is essential to consider the translation requirements early in the process. Appropriate preparation will increase the quality of what you put in and ultimately the quality of what is delivered as a final product.

Most people will intuit what this means when it comes to production. Constructing computers with titanium and other precious metals will increase the quality of the final product. Adding Teflon to a pan immediately increases its value, because the basic components are of higher quality.

But translation is a bit more elusive than something tangible like a computer or pan. When it comes to getting a superior product in translation, what does it mean to be underprepared? How do you know if you are supplying your absolute best materials to the person creating the product of translation?

For one thing, the format in which we receive the content can seriously affect the final product. For example, PDFs, while the most universal documents to share in certain settings, make things incredibly difficult for translators. If you have ever tried to extract text from a PDF by cutting and pasting, then you know, once you cut and paste it into an editing platform, the formatting is completely lost. Symbols, punctuation, and even letters can be altered unintentionally, or omitted in the process, and the workload and timeline will be seriously affected.

This is where our willingness to push back serves our client. If we receive a PDF (in the old days, like in the story above, it could have been a fax), we might take a moment and ask the clients if they have access to the source materials that went into the PDF—an Excel sheet, InDesign file, or Word document. Not only is there less risk of file corruptions and mistakes if we are working directly with the source material, but we use highly specialized tools that will respond to carefully planned formatting, like the use of different fonts, styles, and colors to delineate content. Taking the care to prepare the text at the outset will increase chances of accuracy and create a document that can easily be translated into multiple languages.

When we first started working with AKIKO, we collaborated with their team to improve the quality of source material. Initially, what we were given was in the program PageMaker (it was the nineties, after all). PageMaker was a very common publishing tool at the time, but there was a problem: PageMaker could only be used on their *competitor's computers*. They were not about to buy their competitor's product, so it meant *they themselves* could not read any of the materials being created unless the agency printed them out on paper.

The first thing we did was find a program that

worked on their computers, so that we could all participate in the process. This meant we were now able to pass work back and forth electronically, deal with the absolute raw materials, and allow for a more thorough, accurate, and timely translation. This was just one of the many factors that allowed us trim the turnaround time for their manuals from six weeks to just a couple of days.

"LORENZO CAN DO IT"

Companies often make the mistake of assigning the translation duties to someone who is already on staff. We refer to this as the "Lorenzo can do it" problem. On the surface, it might seem like a commonsense solution—Lorenzo knows your product, he speaks the languages in question, and he's already on your payroll. What could go wrong?

The answer: quite a lot, actually. For one thing, unless Lorenzo was hired for this purpose, any time he spends translating will detract from his duties. He will not prioritize the translation because of competing responsibilities, and this could result in the translation being weeks, if not months, late. When he does prioritize the translation, the rest of his work will suffer. While it might seem appealing to use internal resources because there is "no additional cost," it's a misleading notion. This choice will cost you time and, quite likely, revenue.

Also, despite your employee being a native speaker of the language in question, unless she is a writer, she is unlikely to have formal language skills. Even if she is a writer, what kind of writer is she? Marketing writing, technical writing, and legal writing are all very different and specific crafts. And, as always, translation is much bigger than words on a page. An in-house employee cannot be expected to solve the larger content issues that are sure to arise.

Translation is much bigger than words on a page.

Many companies initially make the "Lorenzo can do it" mistake. And when it inevitably leads to some stumbles, falls, and outright disasters, panic ensues. The project could end up far behind schedule, and because funds have not been allocated for translation (after all, it was all going to be done in-house), executives too often opt for the cheapest, fastest solution, rather than the best solution.

It is never too late to start looking at translation as part of the big picture, the way that we do. If we come on board in a situation like this one, we will start to integrate translation into your journey right away, while utilizing Lorenzo and the work he has already done as an asset. Since he has intimate knowledge of the company, product, and target audience, he is often able to provide useful feedback.

MISAPPLIED TOOLS

Many of our clients are always on the lookout for a magic wand in the form of some sort of software that will solve all their problems. There are plenty of snake oil salesmen who are aware of this and ready to take advantage. I've lost count of the number of boxes of unused software I've seen sitting in our clients' offices, because they just don't do the job. Sometimes a tool can do the job, but the supplier fails to mention the depth of knowledge and training necessary to use it effectively, making it both cost and time prohibitive.

This is especially common when it comes to a large, institutional purchase like a Content Management System (CMS), or a system for Product Information Management (PIM). A CMS or PIM are clearly tools that have far-reaching implications, and many things must be taken into consideration when choosing the right one—usually translated content is just one small component of the overall program. But you might be surprised how often a multilanguage feature is sold as part of the system. Unfortunately, it is often not very effective. It is rare for executives to consider consulting a translation specialist on the usability of multilanguage aspects of a CMS or PIM. But if they would, they might not make a costly mistake.

Software engineers at technology companies *are* master inventors, but they tend to overestimate their ability to solve long-standing problems. Because they are inclined to think in numbers and formulas, they think translation will function similarly. In their eyes, there are few problems in the world that can't be solved through technology.

But translation is more of an art than a science, and it is rarely as simple as plugging words into a program. Imagine if this book that you're reading had to be translated into thirty languages within three weeks. It would be tempting to try to create a technological tool to do it automatically—a computer program you can just run it through, but that would be unrealistic. No matter what, there will be numerous edits, revisions, and nuances. It must all be taken into consideration and built into the workflow; otherwise things are going to fall apart, and quickly.

SILOS

Recently, while looking at an American manufacturing website, we discovered something interesting. From the site, we were able to download a PDF brochure of mechanical data in English, German, and Chinese. As we continued to peruse, we noticed the exact same text that was in the brochure was also on a page of the website, but only in English. Someone had translated the downloadable brochure but did not think or know to share the German and Chinese versions with the people who made the website, despite the fact the text was verbatim and the translations had already been paid for.

This is a clear example of how silos (isolated departments that fail to communicate with each other) can cost your team time and money. A new product might boast an important feature—a Teflon surface, perhaps—and this feature will be highlighted on the website, in internal communications to stakeholders, in the manual, and on the packaging. If departments are not speaking to one another, these claims might be unintentionally translated five separate times, costing the company thousands in extra translation costs. Other times, different departments will use different vendors to translate. So when put through translation, the packaging claim does not correspond to the material that marketing or legal is sending out.

For AKIKO, we translate manuals into more than thirty different languages. The same content from the manuals goes onto a website in an FAQ, and you can be sure we are dealing with different departments when it comes to the manuals and the website. We had to work with the website developers on how to best leverage the work already done in translation and encourage them to not to tinker and make changes. I have often said, adding a single comma will cost you a dollar per language. That might not seem like a lot, but no one adds just a single comma. Once you open the door to those kinds of edits, you are inviting catastrophe. Suddenly, there are hundreds of red marks on the page, adding a semicolon here, changing the capitalization there. If every change is a dollar per language, you might be looking at thousands of dollars, just to add those commas.

When looked at in those terms, people are less likely to quibble over word choice or phrasing but rather see their role as part of the larger story. Over the years everyone at AKIKO has become very disciplined. They only make edits when absolutely necessary, and because we are all working together from the beginning, those last-minute changes rarely happen.

POOR USER JOURNEYS

Part of venturing without a map is translating without really considering *why* you're translating. We see it all the time—clients who have a general idea of what the content should be in English but have not thought about what it should be in different languages, or how to adjust it for different cultures. Because of this, people often end up translating for the sake of translating from some vague idea of necessity, rather than to intentionally grow the international market for their product in a strategic way. This leads to a *poor user journey.*

If you have not put time and thought into what you are translating and why, you may end up with inconsistency in content. In English, a line of bed linens might consistently be called "soft" across all listings, including sheets, pillows, and blankets. But when it gets translated to German, in one place it is translated to "soft," somewhere else, "plush," and somewhere else, "luxurious." In this way, meanings and descriptions can be fickle.

This will also affect online sales. When someone searches the word "soft" on the English site, they might get twenty-one hits. But if someone is searching in German, they might only get six listings under "soft," because the adjective has been interpreted differently in the rest of the listings. This lack of consistency can frustrate users and cost you revenue.

Crafting a reliable, positive user journey comes back to creating that plan—drawing that map to avoid marshy ground. Before you begin translating your products for your website, you must ask, "Are we are going to target France, and what do we want the French user to do before they buy this toaster?" We push our clients by encouraging them to start thinking about *why* a French person in Marseilles should buy their toaster and what the consumer's experience will be like. You cannot assume that everyone buys their toasters from the website like they do in America. In France, people might buy their toasters in supermarkets, in which case they will want to concentrate resources on those ads and displays, rather than online.

Different locations have different user journeys, requiring different content and different translations. When putting a map together, many questions must be asked before you translate a single word. Decisions about content, experience, and culture must all be taken into consideration.

2

COMPLEXITY

NASHVILLE, TENNESSEE, 2018

"It's very simple; our product sells itself," Clark Johnston said in his charming southern accent. "We make the best bourbon in the whole of Tennessee."

"Interesting," said Ian. "Bourbon made in Tennessee. We'll have to think about how to translate that properly."

"Hm. I guess that is a little complicated to an outsider," Clark said. "Anyway, I don't think we have much to talk about today. I just like to shake hands with the people I do business with."

Françoise and Ian were sitting in the large, comfortable office of Johnston Spirits headquarters, and they couldn't help but notice that the ostentatious decor matched Clark's own bombastic tone. A full-size stuffed bear in the corner of the office, posed on his hind legs, as if midroar, distracted Françoise. It was clearly a hunting trophy, and it somehow conveyed a comical and menacing presence at the same time.

"As do we," said Ian. "But I'm afraid there are a few things we do need to discuss."

"It should all be pretty self-explanatory," Clark said dismissively. "We've had a lot of success with our viral campaign here in the States. Did you see that in the files?"

"Yes, we did," said Françoise, looking away from the towering bear. "But we didn't know which sections were meant to be tweets, or what was meant for Facebook, Instagram, or the blog."

"Oh. Well, just translate it all, and our social media people will sort it out," Clark said.

"But there's something you're not considering," Françoise went on. "We need to know which sections are meant for Twitter, because of the character limit."

Clark smiled. "All of the tweets have been measured to be the right number of characters already," he said confidently.

"In German? Or Japanese? The character numbers will change when we translate. It's entirely unpredictable, especially when the alphabet is different."

Clark paused. He clearly had not considered that. "That's a good point."

"Thank you," Françoise said. "And something else. On the website, you are translating programming that restricts who can enter. It limits visitors to those over twenty-one years of age."

"That's right."

"Well, America is one of very few places in the world where the drinking age is twenty-one. And even in the US, not every state adheres to this."

"Oh. So, should we change it to eighteen?" asked Clark.

"For most places. But there are exceptions. In parts of Canada the drinking age is nineteen. In Japan, it is twenty. In Cuba, it is sixteen. And in many places, there is no drinking age at all, only restrictions on buying alcohol."

Clark looked at Françoise wide-eyed, surprised by her vast knowledge of drinking ages around the world. She shrugged. "We travel a lot."

"So, you can see," Ian continued, "there will be many variations for the languages and countries the website is destined for."

"Yes, I see. Well." Clark leaned back in his chair. He seemed almost afraid to ask it. "Anything else?"

"As long as we're on the subject," Ian said, "I notice you want us to translate in Arabic, but I think we should talk about it before we do."

"Why is that? Aren't there a lot of people in the Middle East?"

"Certainly, but there is not a lot of public drinking. In some countries drinking is outlawed altogether, and for the others, well…" Ian parsed his thoughts carefully. "I'm not sure how a drink hailed as an all-American spirit will be received."

"I see."

"We should at least determine in which countries in the Middle East you plan on marketing. That will help our precision," Ian said.

"We will translate everything, of course. Whatever you want," Françoise assured him. "We just don't want you to spend money on something that won't end up being useful to you."

"And I certainly appreciate that," Clark said. "I guess there are some complications that we hadn't anticipated."

"It is usually more complex than it looks," Ian agreed.

"I just thought we needed a good translator."

"Well, this is what a good translator will do for you," said Françoise. "We could just translate the words and send them back to you, but that wouldn't be doing you a service. We want to make sure you are truly getting what you pay for."

"You know what?" Clark reached into his desk drawer and pulled out a bottle of bourbon and three glasses. He opened the bottle and began to pour. "That is something I think we can all drink to."

He passed out the bourbon. The delicious scent of pure Tennessee bourbon filled the air. Ian raised his glass. "I guess this won't be simple after all," Clark said. "So here's to solving complex problems and sharing bourbon with the world!"

They all clinked their glasses and drank.

COMPLEXITY

One of the things we want to communicate on our quest is just how complex translation can be. It's one thing to say, over and over again, "It's about content, not just linguistics," but what does that actually mean? How does it affect the way things are translated, and how does it impact the ways in which your company can plan ahead?

Complexity is not inherently a bad thing. In our

modern world we want everything simple, quick, and automatic. People have lost their patience for intricate problem solving, and so when they hear that something is "complex," they immediately get nervous. For a company executive, "complex" might be synonymous with "expensive" or "time draining."

> The complexity of translation is part of the process. It does not have to be problem inducing, or frustrating, or even expensive. But it must be understood.

However, in our years of working with clients, we have come to understand that the complexity of translation is part of the process. It does not have to be problem inducing, or frustrating, or even expensive. But it must be understood.

There are many factors that contribute to the complexity of a project; some can be predicted, and some cannot. Over the years, we have developed an innate understanding of the common challenges that arise when working in translation. We know the usual suspects, but there is always something that we have never come across before, something specific to the client's project. That said, there are several things to think about before embarking on a translation journey that will help you anticipate complexities and plan for their eventuality.

DESTINATIONS, RESTRICTIONS, AND LEGISLATIONS

As is illustrated in the above anecdote about Johnston Spirits, clients have to think about the final destination for their product. Translating words and content will change the length and look of the work. Not only must you consider the number of characters for an application like Twitter, but also what image are you using on Instagram or Facebook? Will it have cultural resonance outside of the United States? Will there be controversy you weren't anticipating? You can't know what you don't know, but you can be sure that things will be more complicated than they seem on the outset.

Every year, we work with Wikipedia by donating our services to Wiki Medicine. Over the years, we have picked different themes to translate, things like hygiene and neglected tropical diseases. One year we chose to focus on female health, and suddenly, what had always been a straightforward translation project became very complex as the conversation over what content was translated turned contentious.

As a company based in the West, our view of female health diverts from other cultures. There are different views and even laws about what you can and cannot put online in many places in the world, and so we could not *simply* translate the English text we were given. Hygiene had been simple—it wasn't going to be as easy to wash our hands of this one (pun intended).

Sometimes, when considering the destination of your content, there may be more work than you anticipated. Let's say you're translating your retail website into German. It seems simple at first—translate the product names and information, the costs, the shipping information. So, you send the existing website to your translator to extract the English content and translate to German.

But what happens when you have a German customer who visits your website and has a question? You're not going to answer it in English, so what's the mechanism for dealing with that German inquiry, which is coming in via email, live chat, or by telephone? And if you are going to provide a live chat or telephone customer service, you have to consider the time zone, because most Germans are visiting during German business hours, not US business hours. So, just by translating your website into German, which is an easy enough exercise, a new set of questions and challenges are uncovered.

Now consider the fact that you are translating that website into ten more languages for nineteen more countries. Each of those destinations and all of their restrictions and laws need to be considered when you put your legal, tax, and contact information onto your website. Suddenly the whole endeavor is far more intricate than first thought.

One year our client Destinations Worldwide developed a charming little calendar as a promotional item. Because it was developed and printed in America, it had the predictable identifications for the days of the week: S(unday)-M(onday)-T(uesday)-W(ednesday)-T(hursday)-F(riday)-S(aturday)—initials that will be immediately recognizable to the English-speaking world.

Our clients couldn't understand why this promotion wasn't working for the Chinese. What they hadn't accounted for was that in China, the days of the week are translated into numbers, as in D(ay 1), D(ay 2), D(ay 3), and so on. So, the calendar, looked bizarre and confusing with D-D-D everywhere. The initials of the days of the week were meaningless, and the whole endeavor was completely confounding to their Chinese audience.

In the end, the translation required a change to

something very elemental. In this case, the change came at a late stage, after design and production, so it became very costly for them to retrofit. It was a fundamental content mistake, a poor job by the previous translation company, who should have thought more carefully about how the translations would be used.

TO KEEP IT SIMPLE, EMBRACE THE COMPLEXITY

Here's the good news: if a translator has had the right experience and shares the core belief that translation is about communication of content, they will already be thinking two or three steps ahead. Part of the translator's job is anticipating the complex questions that are sure to arise. The sooner you involve them in the conversation, the sooner they can help you uncover the hidden complexities so you can make informed decisions.

It is important to think beyond your current project and into the future—to anticipate how the translation today might affect what you want to do a year, three years, or five years down the road. If you can look that far into the future, it will help you shape your content today.

Even if you don't realize it, the project you are

working on today can have serious implications for your company down the road. Something that you expect to be a one-off job might end up being the foundation of a campaign that will go on for the next ten years. If you have not spent the proper time preparing and vetting the project, you might find yourself stuck with a creaky foundation on which to build your empire.

The goal is to provide you scalable solutions for your content needs and your content problems. One thing we suggest is to run a pilot project. Creating a test model that does not have the same stakes as an official project will allow you to gain a lot of valuable insight into what will happen once everything is scaled up.

On our team, we have global content business process analysts who are ready to get into the complex, nitty-gritty of what it means to sell your product to an international audience. Even if all you are doing is translating materials for an executive who's going on a business trip to China, it can't hurt to take a moment to consider, What will come of this? If all you need is to translate her business cards, you probably won't have a scalability problem. But what if she is successful in her negotiations? What's the commitment coming out of this trip? What is the tone and language surrounding the deal? All of this might have long-term implications, and there are complexities that are well hidden when her flights are first booked.

A lot of what we will discuss in this book will be specific, detailed efforts to make complexity more transparent. When we talk about things like marshy ground, or the various ways you can find yourself in the weeds, it is often a more specific way or detailing the complexity that went unforeseen. The first step is to internalize the knowledge that translation is about more that words—it's a content issue. Beyond that, it is about finding the right partner to help you foresee the complexities of communicating your message to a global audience—finding "a good translator" to help you navigate the way.

3

WHO WE ARE

EDINBURGH, SCOTLAND, 1994

Ian and Françoise sat across from each other in the charming old café they often visited for lunch. Around them, noise and chaos from the afternoon rush filled the room, yet the two of them were at a loss for words.

It was a cozy little place where the food was good and the atmosphere friendly. The walls were lined with shelves, which were filled with books and board games. The management didn't seem to mind if people picked up a novel to read, gathered around a game to play, or just sat to chat for hours.

Ian and Françoise were testing this theory—they had been there for hours. They weren't reading or playing a game. They weren't even eating; their lunches had barely been touched. They were both deep in thought. Finally, Françoise broke the silence.

"It has to be something simple," she reiterated.

"Yes."

"But clever."

"Of course."

"And easy to remember."

"Right."

"But not too obvious."

Ian sat back in his chair with a sigh. "Yes. All of those things. You'll get no argument from me," he said. "But what?"

It was not the first time they had discussed it, nor was it the first time they found themselves stuck. They had decided on many things: the timing was right, they knew what they wanted to do, when they were going to do it, why, and where. All they needed to finalize was their name. Who were they going to be?

"I hadn't anticipated it being this hard," Françoise said, picking at her salad with a fork. "Of all the aspects of starting a business…naming it has stumped us."

"And our business is one of words."

"Yes, but that's the thing, it's about so much more

than words. That's why we can't call it something like 'TechSpeak.' Or 'Lingo.' Something too on-the-nose lacks imagination and creativity. Not to mention, being too literal misrepresents the whole endeavor of translation."

"Yes, but we also can't call it something too poetic, like 'Impressions,'" Ian said, reminding her of one of their previous, weaker offerings.

Françoise groaned. "Sounds like a soap opera."

"Yes, and we're trying to be drama free," laughed Ian. "No acronyms, because no one will know what we're talking about."

"Can't be too technical," she went on, almost to herself. "Can't be too basic."

She tapped her fingers on the table absentmindedly and looked out the window. There was a chill in the air, and a light rain had begun to fall.

"Having regrets?" she heard Ian ask.

"No!" she answered. "Not at all. There are challenges to this sort of thing. But we're up for it. It's just not time to break out the champagne. Yet."

It had been several weeks since she had come home from her long-awaited vacation and saw the blinking red light on her answering machine. It was Ian's message. The one she hadn't realized she was waiting for. After she had quit Q Translations, and he had been given her job, she had been too busy as a freelance translator to give it much more thought.

But then, she was standing in her living room, fresh off the ferry. The relaxation she felt from her holiday evaporated into excitement as she listened to his voice on the line. "I've had enough. I've quit as well," he had said. "I think we should go for it." And then he hung up. It was just as well—he didn't need to say anything else. She knew what he meant, and she was ready to take the leap together.

Both had come to the conclusion that the work being done at Q Translations was no longer something to which they could attach their names. Both shared the philosophy that would be the bedrock of their new business endeavor—translation must be approached as an issue of overall content, not just word for word interpretation. Both wanted to approach each project as an opportunity to build a relationship, not just a one-off job. They would create something different, a new kind of business.

A spark lit up Françoise's eyes. The red blinking light. The new world order.

"Wait a minute."

She got up, and Ian watched as she zigzagged between tables and chairs, avoiding other patrons. She got to one of the bookshelves and scanned it quickly, then pulled a huge, well-worn book off the shelf. She turned and headed back to their table.

"They've always got one, for the folks who want to play Scrabble!" she said with a wink.

"What is it?" Ian asked with interest.

She held up the spine so he could see—it was a classic Oxford dictionary.

"That looks ancient!" he exclaimed.

"That's all right. The word I'm looking for is ancient as well."

She flipped through the onion skin–like pages. She landed on what she was looking for, read it quickly, and looked up in triumph. "I've got it."

Her enthusiasm was infectious. "What is it?" Ian said, almost breathless.

She held out the dictionary for him to see. "Rubric."

"Of course," he said. It was just the sort of name they were looking for. It had several connotations— the red markings of an important note made on a document, the term used for an established custom or tradition, a designation of classification, an explanation or comment. Each meaning had a literal or figurative relationship to what they were doing and how they were approaching their new business.

"Another thing that they don't mention here,"

said Ian, handing the book back to her. "It's what the Romans called it when they would introduce new, important legislation."

Françoise smiled. "That's right. A new way of doing things."

"It's perfect," Ian said. "It's not a word-for-word explanation of what we do, but the communication of a concept."

"Done!" Françoise was excited, closing the dictionary with a snap.

"Not just yet," he said. "I still have to check with the Companies House to make sure it's available."

"It will be," said a confident Françoise. "Arnold!" she suddenly called out to the young man who had been serving them all afternoon. He heard her and began to make his way over.

"Françoise, how can you be so sure?"

"Well, I'm not really," she admitted, taking a big bite of her salad. "But I have a feeling it will be."

"And why is that?"

"Because it's the right one."

Ian laughed and turned to Arnold who had arrived at their table. "Please, bring the lady some champagne!"

OUR ORIGIN STORY

Every great adventure or quest begins with an origin story. Ours might not be as action packed as those in *Captain America* or *Black Panther*, but it does illustrate how we arrived where we are, and how we amassed important knowledge along the way.

My background is in technology. Early in my career, my work in the oil industry took me all over the world—far from my native Denmark to places like Nigeria, Cameroon, and Oman. I spent years in Germany and then New Zealand. Eventually I ended up in the UK, doing technology-driven sales for a translation company called Q Translations. Q Translations was a company based in Ireland, but they hired me to work in their UK office, which had been set up to cater to Fotonz, an American technology company that did a lot of business in the UK. This is where I met Françoise.

Françoise had grown up in France and had studied language throughout her academic career. She always had a passion for languages and especially the creative process of translation. She had settled in the UK young and worked as a freelance translator for years, building an impressive roster of clients, including Fotonz. When they wanted to expand operations, they decided to work with Q Translations—a large company that they thought would be equipped to handle their growth. But because they loved Françoise and the work she did, they made sure she was hired to set up the UK office for Q Translations. Within a year the office was busy, catering to all of Fotonz's needs, with a staff of twenty translators. At a certain point, they were so efficient, they decided they could take on more work and seek out new clients. So, they decided to hire a salesperson. Guess who that was.

For a while it was great. With Françoise as the boss, and me bringing in new business, the office in the UK grew rapidly. The office in Ireland was also busy, so for the most part we were left to our own devices. It was clear that Françoise and I made an excellent team, and we began to develop our philosophy in those early days of working together.

But soon, the work in the Ireland office began to dry up, and they started looking at us to use their services to fulfill *our* customers' needs. This took the control of the process out of our hands, and we started to see deterioration in the quality of the service. That's when Françoise left. And, after a very brief period, I followed her. It wasn't what I wanted to be doing, or how I wanted to do it, and the person I wanted to work with most had walked out the door. We both knew it was time for us to venture out on our own. And so, Rubric was born.

It only took us a few months to be in working order (after years of working in business, choosing a name proved to be one of the hardest parts). In fact, on the very first day of Rubric's operations, we were contacted by one of the clients we had worked with at Q Translations. They were working with our former employers in Ireland, but had found themselves in a real pickle. Q Translations was working on translating a product manual for a roll out in Europe, but they had essentially "ghosted" them (to use a twenty-first-century term). The work was just not being done, the Ireland office was being noncommunicative, and the holdup was causing major problems.

The company? AKIKO. We were hired, and we hadn't even gone looking for them. They came to us.

In fact, we were scrupulous about not going on a fishing expedition for former clients. We wanted to respect boundaries and run a clean business. But it didn't matter. Q Translations and other companies like them really did our work for us by failing to communicate with their clients.

So, we had secured a major client on day one of Rubric's operations. Needless to say, we were excited, but we also had our work cut out for us. I will never forget that first trip we took to the AKIKO headquarters. We went to their office, and the image of what I saw was imprinted in my mind: hundreds and hundreds of computer boxes, each with a label that said, "AWAITING MANUAL." They had the product ready to go, but the delay in translation was costing them time and money. They had so many computers awaiting manuals they had to rent trucks to park outside of their office just to store them all.

First Guiding Principle: No matter what, we never leave a client hanging.

This experience helped us form one of our main guiding principles: No matter what, we never leave a client hanging. There is nothing worse than having product that is ready to go, and just waiting for a translation.

AKIKO did not want to alert Q Translations that they had made alternative plans, as they still had a lot of sensitive material and other projects in the pipeline with them. That left us in an awkward position. We had none of the original documents or source materials to work with, as Q Translations had gone dark. We ended up having to reverse-engineer previously translated materials from Adobe PostScript (PDF's predecessor) and add in the new information to reflect the new product.

The difficulty of this task helped us form the second of our main guiding principles: a client should never lack access to their own intellectual property. Whenever we work with a client, we hand all the working materials over to them.

> **Second Guiding Principle: A client should never lack access to their own intellectual property.**

A famous computer software company used to have a saying: you're only as good as your last five minutes. We live by that. Knowing that our clients could leave us at any time keeps us on our toes and striving to provide them with excellent service.

That excellent service was our mission from day one, and we demonstrated to the executives at AKIKO that even in extreme conditions, we could outperform our previous employer. It took us six weeks to get their manuals translated and finished in four languages, in which time Q Translations had barely been in touch with them. When AKIKO finally heard from Q Translations, they were contrite and understanding. They had botched it, and we had risen to the occasion.

This helped us form a third guiding principle: we owe our clients honesty. We value transparency and communication, and if there is a problem, the first thing we do is talk to them.

Third Guiding Principle: We owe our clients honesty.

It's extremely rare, but occasionally there will be a problem or delay—after all, we don't live in a perfect world. But we never ghost them or go dark. We touch base and talk through the issue. Sometimes they themselves already have the solution.

All of this was twenty-five years ago, but we have never forgotten that feeling—the thrill of solving a problem, of meeting a challenge head on. It left us with so much energy, and we still often find those adrenalin rushes keep us going. We love solving problems. Clients come to us not only because we deliver a superior product, but also because we thrive in difficult situations and solve issues in unorthodox ways when necessary. We hate wasting time—either our clients' or our own—and we're always searching for efficient solutions.

Fourth Guiding Principle: There is no problem that can't be solved.

A fourth and final guiding principle that we took from the AKIKO experience: there is no problem that can't be solved.

I would say, "The rest is history," but it's all still going on. We have added many, many clients, of course, but we still work with AKIKO. They have gone through enormous changes in the last twenty-five years—they've grown to be a multibillion-dollar company, and they've expanded their product line. But one thing that has always stayed constant is our working relationship. The people we work with keep us on because they know we provide the very best services in the industry. You might even say it's our rubric.

SILOS

MILAN, ITALY, 2010

Silvia and Ian were walking down a tree-lined street near Dallow-Klein's European headquarters. It was a beautiful spring day in Milan, and signs of life were emerging everywhere after a long, cold winter.

Ian looked over at Silvia. Her face was still fixed in the same concerned, concentrated mask she had when he arrived for their meeting half an hour ago. The Dallow-Klein offices were smart and sleek—conducive to getting work done, but his years of experience with clients immediately told him she needed a change of scenery.

"Let's get some fresh air," he had suggested before sitting down, and she had jumped at the chance.

Now he could see that whatever was weighing on her, a brisk walk wasn't going to fix it. He wasn't sure what was on her mind, and she wasn't yet giving any clues. Silvia had joined the Dallow-Klein team only eight months prior, and she had hired Rubric shortly after that. In their time working together, she was always very forthright, and it seemed unlike her to be evasive. As one of the youngest project managers in the company, she was hardworking and fastidious. She seemed determined to prove herself, especially in her first big assignment. They had put her in charge of the European rollout of their new personal hygiene product: an apple-scented shampoo called Apple Crisp. It had been a big hit with the US market, and they expected a smooth launch. She brought Rubric on board to do the translations.

But they were met with problems no one had anticipated. They had just begun working on the translations when Françoise noticed that the ingredient list supplied for the advertisements was different from the list supplied for the labels on the bottle. The former had come from the marketing department, the latter from production. When she brought this to

Silvia's attention, they had discovered that the formula had been changed because certain ingredients used in the original were banned in Europe. No one had bothered to tell the marketing department.

Upon further digging, they discovered the social media manager in Milan had been teasing the product launch online for months. He had already translated sections of the American marketing for use on blogs, Twitter, Facebook, and Instagram, including the claim, "Apple Crisp smells more like fresh fruit than any other shampoo!" This was a claim that tested well in US markets, but it couldn't be used in Germany or France without being vetted by the legal department. He hadn't spoken to anyone before taking it upon himself to translate the claims.

It was a real mess, but when many other managers would have panicked, Silvia had handled the situation expertly. Leaning on Ian's and Françoise's expertise, she had pulled everyone onto the same page and managed to launch the product on time, with a consistent message.

So, why did she look like she had bit into a lemon when she should have been celebrating?

"What's on your mind?" he asked.

"Can we sit?" She pointed at a bench and sat before waiting for an answer. Ian sat next to her, and they were both quiet for a moment, looking out onto a busy street.

"I've been thinking about apple shampoo," she said.

Ian laughed. "Tell me about it! Every time I taste an apple, I think about how it would make my hair shiny and clean."

"But seriously," said Silvia. "I am concerned."

"The launch went well," said Ian. "Aren't we meeting to talk about your next project?"

"Yes, but that's just it," she said, shaking her head. "I'm worried about the next one."

"Why?"

"It's just that, with Apple Crisp, as soon as we looked past the surface, there were all these cracks showing," she said. "Who's to say it won't happen again?"

"Oh, it probably will," said Ian offhandedly.

"What? Do you mean it?"

"Yes, it's quite likely. It happens with almost every product, to some extent," Ian admitted. "Françoise and I see it a lot, especially in the bigger companies with presence in multiple countries. We call it the 'Silo Problem.'"

"That's it, exactly!" Exclaimed Silvia. "Everyone is operating independently of each other, as though we were separated into silos."

"It's common," said Ian almost apologetically.

"And is there no solution?"

"Well, Françoise and I have often hypothesized that the only real solution would be for companies to hire a chief global content officer. Someone who is coordinating all aspects of the content from one department to another. But you never see that."

"Why not?" asked Silvia with a new enthusiasm. "There are chief financial officers. chief marketing officers. There's a global officer for sales and brand management. Why not content management?"

Ian shrugged. "It would go a long way to solve the problem caused by silos," he said. "But most companies just don't seem to recognize the need."

"Well, then," said Silvia, reinvigorated. "That's what my next project must be!"

She stood up quickly and began walking back the way they had come. Ian barely knew what had happened. He remained dumbfounded, sitting on the bench. She looked back at him. "Are you coming?"

He got up and jogged to catch up with her.

"Sorry, I missed something. What is your next project?"

Now she was walking at a quick and determined pace back toward the office.

"Talking the Dallow-Klein executives into hiring a chief global content officer."

Ian laughed. "You make it sound so easy."

"Oh, I am sure it will be quite difficult. Any major change like this is brutal to put into action," she admitted. "Especially when it is being proposed by someone so new to the company. But"—and now she stopped in the middle of the sidewalk to look at him—"will it be any harder than dealing with these problems over and over again every time we launch a new product? No," she decided, and then began walking again. "I would rather fight this fight now, and make real change in the company. Otherwise, I'll just be facing the same 'Silo Problems' for the next twenty years. A chief global content officer, it is!"

"Well, it's a superb idea," he agreed.

She looked at him, finally a smile on her face. "It's your idea! I'm just the one who will make it happen at Dallow-Klein."

THE SILO PROBLEM

In chapter 1, we touched on silos and how they can land a project in marshy ground. It's a common problem that can manifest in many different ways and create major, costly delays. So, what causes silos?

Why are they so common and what are some ways they can be addressed?

COMPANY CULTURE

Sometimes it is company policy or company culture that leads to the construction of silos. We often encounter the attitude of, "This is the way things have always been done, and we're not going to change it now." It's not an unreasonable position, in theory. If a multimillion- or multibillion-dollar company has gotten this far, it's safe to assume their team is doing something very right. However, putting your product onto the global market changes things immediately, and there will be new challenges that require adjustments.

The story of Dallow-Klein's Apple Crisp shampoo illustrates how even the most straightforward projects can have unanticipated problems arise. For each different product there may be many

Even the most straightforward projects can have unanticipated problems arise.

new aspects to consider. What are the claims being made by marketing? What are the ingredients included in the product? What kind of warnings must be included for use? What effect will use have on the environment? What are the possible effects of the product on health? Tracking the changes in content from country to country can be overwhelming, and when there are silos in the mix, mistakes can be made and important requirements can be overlooked. The results can be fines, delays, and headaches.

There may be company policies in place to avoid breaking antitrust laws. Keeping up walls internally might help prevent conflict of interest. Sometimes policies are maintained because when one company acquired another, they allowed them to maintain independence and their own company culture. This might have helped them preserve their team morale and high performance, but it can also lead to the building of silos.

Company culture and policies can be the hardest to change. Not everyone has a Silvia on their team to take on the problem and advocate for a solution with the higher-ups. But there are small steps that can be taken to begin to address these customs, and we will discuss them more at the end of the chapter.

EMPIRE BUILDING

In extremely large companies, we sometimes see the deliberate construction of silos. People might harbor concerns that a more streamlined process will make their own jobs obsolete. Sometimes ceding control does mean giving part of their territory away. And as a result, you might begin to see competing departments; you might see distributors in different countries not wanting to work together; or you might see a marketing team in Belgium refuse to communicate with the marketing team in Japan, because they've conveniently decided their audiences are just too different, and they cannot share content.

When we worked with Dogomu, a Japanese technology company, we ran into these self-defeating problems. Most of their production goes to southeast Asia, so their most important markets are Japan, China, and Korea, but they do have a presence in the US and Europe. Unlike English, translating from Japanese into any other language is very expensive (the exception being translating Japanese into Chinese or Korean, which is comparatively cheap). To keep costs down, they first translated their content into English, and then translated into all other languages from that document.

Or at least, that was the plan. Because Dogomu

used internal Japanese translators, their English documents could sometimes be rough, which led the US office to become frustrated. Rather than communicate with Japan and formulate a plan to work together, the Americans just rewrote the documentation before then sending it out to translation.

So, the Americans were not willing to adopt the Japanese manual, and they wouldn't share their rewrites, which could have been very helpful to us. Now there are silos being built inside silos: The Japanese were translating into English, the Americans were rewriting the English for their country, meanwhile the Europeans were using the English version from Japan to translate into Spanish and French. On the other hand, Mexico used the American version to translate into Spanish. And why did the Mexicans need to retranslate the manual into Spanish from the American manual, when a (Japanese English) Spanish version already existed?

It became a huge mess because no one was talking to each other, and everyone wanted to be responsible for themselves, and themselves alone. Whether they were trying to protect the integrity of the product or their own jobs, it's the kind of empire building that ultimately serves no one.

We have definitely seen companies overcome this

problem. AKIKO is a good example. The way they work is the opposite of a silo. They have a central communications hub in Germany, through which everything flows. It's a model we encourage in the companies we work with, but it cannot be achieved overnight.

TRANSLATION REAL ESTATE

Silos and their effect can also be the result of how much "real estate" is claimed by translation—the bigger the company, the less real estate, and the larger the silo effect.

What does this mean? Well, if a company is small, in the fifty- to a hundred-million-dollar range, the amount of the budget that is spent on translation might be visible right up to a VP level. There might be discussions and plans made in the C-suite in order to budget and prepare, and so the silo effect might be minimized.

However, for a billion-dollar company, translation expenditures are likely so far down the list that there's nobody overseeing the overall process. Combine that with a fundamental misunderstanding of translation as a linguistic issue rather than a content issue, and it can very much get lost into the different silos.

For some company executives, planning for translation seems like buying glue and paper clips—they're thinking about it as something individualized to each department. But this is a mistake, as we have seen time and time again. The impact of translation affects the company across departments and should therefore be considered at a company-wide level.

BASIC CONFUSION

It is easy for us to identify silos as a problem, because we are continually coming up against them in our work. But most executives are not thinking in terms of silos—most don't even know they exist.

When a company like Dallow-Klein puts out their Apple Crisp shampoo, they may have up to five separate sources of content. There is marketing, communications, technical, legal, packaging. And for the most part they are not talking to each other. They may not have a sense of where their work intersects, and how there may be redundancies in translations and beyond.

These problems of ignorance and confusion are par for the course and can only be recognized and fixed with experience. Françoise and I know this, because we have come up against it often in our working life, and have made many of our own mistakes.

In our early days of working with AKIKO, we used to save the translated files on floppy disks and send them to the printers that way. At first, we assumed that it would be easier for the printers if we cut the books into individual chapters, because each chapter would be a smaller file. So, we would create the whole book, and then we would cut it into chapters, save them all on separate disks, and then send the disks to AKIKO and their printers.

At a certain point, we had to discuss something with the printers directly, and we discovered that the printers were just saving the files from the disks on their computers, and then stitching the chapters back together in one document as soon as they got them! Because we hadn't consulted on this, we were all putting meaningless work in on opposite ends of the process.

This is an example of a silo outside of the company structure, but a silo nonetheless. We learned an important lesson from this: all parties must be speaking to each other for full transparency.

SOLUTIONS—TAKING DOWN THE SILO WALLS

Silos will not go away on their own, and the importance of content oversight is only going to grow as time goes on. In the past, the product was what drove sales. You would develop a unique product and people would buy it based on their need. Now, a unique product will have been copied and imitated multiple times within a few months of launch, making the actual product and consumer need less important than the content and message surrounding the product.

Think about our relationship to cars: in the past, people were wedded to their limited options within their price range. Now, there are countless options, so people are making decisions based on the messaging. "I'm a person who drives a Lexus," or "I see myself in a Range Rover." It's about the image of the product, and that's all about the content of the message.

Consistency of message has never been more important, but not every company is ready to create the position of chief global content officer. So, what can be done to address the issue of silos immediately?

Encouraging better communication is a good start. For example, after the AKIKO printing debacle, we learned our lesson. Now, one of the first questions that we ask our client is, "When you receive translated files from us, what happens to them? What is your process?" Not only is it a brief question that can save everyone hours and hours of manpower, but we still make new discoveries with each new client. We continually find out that simple adjustments, at their end or at ours, make everyone's life much easier.

Once we are embedded with a company, we also begin to break the walls between the silos ourselves. With the help of executives, we organize workshops to speak to different departments. We'll engage different teams who don't usually interact, and help explain what they do, their process, and how we've made it easier for them. Then, a few weeks later, we're talking to a new team.

Asking questions, taking the time to investigate, providing organized processes—this is what sets us apart from other translation services. If you are just looking for a one-off translation project, then most companies in the industry are the same. But the reason we care about silos, the reason we ask our questions, is because we plan to come on board for life. We

> **Asking questions, taking the time to investigate, providing organized processes— this is what sets us apart from other translation services.**

know once you work with us, you will want us on multiple projects, and because of this we are constantly in conversation with our client in how we can improve the process for next time.

And of course, like everything else, it is essential to understand translation as a larger content issue, rather than just a matter of linguistics for each department to solve on their own. Translation should not be siloed but must be integrated into the process of development from the very beginning.

This is an adjustment for many executives for whom the idea of translation is mostly transactional. "I need this translated, you do it, and come back to me when you're done." We often begin our relationships that way, but once we have established a rapport, we will return to our contacts as say, "OK. This time, maybe we should do it a little bit differently because it will be to your and our advantage to do so."

Silos are not a new problem, and they are not going to disappear overnight. But when they are approached with foresight and experience, they can be dealt with and eventually even dismantled.

GETTING OUT WHAT YOU PUT IN

EDINBURGH, SCOTLAND, 2015

"What time is it?"

"Hm?"

"What time is it?" Micah repeated. "I turned the clock on my computer off."

Ian looked at his watch. It was only then he realized how tired his eyes were. He rolled his sore shoulders and tried to shake himself more awake. He turned to answer Micah, who was sitting across the room, looking disheveled. Before he could say the time, Françoise chimed in.

"Don't tell me; I don't want to know."

"I'm just wondering if it's time for more coffee," Micah offered, standing up with a stretch.

"Well, the answer to that is yes," Françoise proclaimed, handing him her mug. Micah took it, smiling wearily but genuinely.

"I'll put on another pot."

He left the room and Françoise turned to Ian. "OK, so what time is it?"

Ian laughed. "It's eleven fifteen."

Françoise suddenly snapped to attention. "Really?" She scooted her chair over next to his. "Well, Micah has finished the conclusion, and I'm nearly done with the index—just four more lines to check. You?"

"I've been done for twenty minutes. I'm just checking Facebook."

Françoise slapped his arm playfully. "I'm serious."

"I'm done, I'm done! Just finished," he laughed and showed her the computer screen.

She looked at him wide eyed. "What are you saying? Are you saying we've done it?"

"If you get back over there and finish the index, then it looks like we have," he answered.

She quickly rolled back over to her computer and

78

got back to work. He looked out the window. It was a sunny morning, and the last thing he wanted was another cup of coffee, but it was good for Micah to be up from his desk. The poor fellow had been working nonstop, and he wanted to be sure everything was finished before he broke the news.

They had been working on the Brower Electronics training manuals for six weeks. In three weeks, over a thousand conference attendees would be arriving in Nice, France, for a week-long conference and training session on Brower's major new releases: a gaming console, smart home device, and TV streaming system. The items would initially be launched in the United States and France before a larger worldwide rollout. Rubric had been hired to translate three two-hundred-page training manuals—one for each of the new product lines.

From the very beginning it had been a complicated process. The Brower communications department had sent them the files in Word, but there were a number of formatting problems, and many images they needed to account for. Françoise had requested the files be re-sent in InDesign, and though the team had happily obliged, it had slowed the process down.

Still, they had made it work. By working closely with both the marketing and engineering team, and by bringing on Micah to help oversee a team of translators, they were able to get the manuals translated and ready for print. And not a moment too soon—in order for them to have the manuals ready for the conference, they would need to have them to the printers no later than Tuesday at noon. On Monday, at about six o'clock in the evening, they had finished their work and declared it ready for print. They sent everyone else home, and Ian, Françoise, and Micah broke out the bubbly, ready to toast a job well done.

Then, the email came in.

"We've made some last-minute changes to the English version of the TV streaming manual," it read. "We've listed them in the attached PDF. Can you make them in the French version as well?"

Ian's heart sank as he opened the PDF and saw pages upon pages of changes. Some were as minute as a comma, some as large as a replacement photo and caption.

"They can't be serious," Micah said, his panic mounting. "They're joking."

Ian and Françoise looked at each other. They knew it was no joke. "I'm afraid not," Ian said.

Micah looked incredulous. "But it took us months to get it all done. All of these changes? We'll never be able to do it by noon tomorrow," he shook his head and sat down. "And if we don't finish the streaming manual, then there's no point in sending the other two. The whole thing has fallen apart!"

"All right, no need to be dramatic," Françoise said, her mind already unpacking the problem. She turned to Ian. "We can't do it like this, comparing the PDF to the document. If they have a list of the changes—"

"Then they must have already made them in the InDesign file of the English version," Ian said, finishing her thought. "They should send us the final English file, and we'll translate it through our software."

"We did that already!" Micah said, coming a bit unraveled.

"So, we'll do it again," said Françoise.

Micah looked at his watch. "In eighteen hours?"

Ian and Françoise both shrugged. "Where's your sense of adventure?" Ian asked, and they got to work.

Now, it was the next morning, and after no sleep, ten pots of coffee, and a middle-of-the-night singalong to "Thunder Road," by Bruce Springsteen, they had actually pulled it off. The files were ready to go and would be printed on time.

"Finished!" exclaimed Françoise from across the room. She looked up at Ian. "It's done."

"That may have been the hardest I've ever worked in my life," said Ian. "And I never want to do it again."

"Me neither! So, how do we avoid this happening?"

Ian sat back thoughtfully. "There's nothing we can really do. It's up to the client to make sure we get the right materials."

"You get out what you put in," Françoise agreed. "We'll have to spread the word."

"We'll print bumper stickers. But perhaps we should send this to the printers first?"

"Yes," said Françoise. "Micah!" she called into the kitchen. "It's time!"

GETTING OUT WHAT YOU PUT IN

We've all heard of the medieval art of alchemy. Before we understood complex concepts of chemistry and matter, alchemists thought that with the right process, they could turn lead into gold. We now understand that there are certain physical properties you simply cannot change, and the quality of the matter you put in for the most part is the same quality you will get out.

This wisdom does not always carry over to the translation sphere. It's not that clients don't *want* to provide us with the highest-quality materials—it's just that, for the most part, no one has clarified what it *means* to provide high-quality materials. Our clients are busy and don't always have an intrinsic understanding of what it means to translate, and usually no one has taken the time to explain it to them.

One thing that you must understand is that translators use highly specialized programs to translate. When you combine those programs, excellent translators, and very polished materials, you will have a seamless, high-quality translation, delivered on time. We provide two out of three of those elements, but the third—finished materials—is up to our client to provide. This chapter will give you some insight into why this can be hard to do, and provide some solutions to the problem.

UNFINISHED DOCUMENTS

Many times, when we receive a document for translation, we find there are still notes in the margin not meant for us. "Check with legal" or "Update this wording." This is usually a sign that it is too early for us to be translating, as things are likely to change. If something needs to be checked with legal or wording needs to be updated, then there is no point in us translating it before that happens. Don't forget, it may only be a simple change in English, an adjustment of "his" to "their," for example, but if you are talking about translating it into fifteen languages, you can multiply that work by fifteen. The room for error and the cost are increased significantly at that point.

Sometimes, changes are simply unavoidable. That is a fact of life and one we are ready for. Those inevitable yet unpredictable adjustments are all the more reason to make sure that materials sent to the translator are as complete as possible. What might save time on the supply end will end up costing time and money on the translation end.

If the volume of work is very significant, we might need to see drafts in order to prepare and get started. As long as it is made clear that we are working with a draft of the document, having access to unfinished material gives us a head start. The problem is, most of the time, people who send us the document don't *know* it's a draft. Even if there aren't tracked changes or notes in the margin, adjustments will still come in. This is often because someone in the company is fiddling around in English, and making changes that, to their mind, make no real impact. Someone will change "which" to "that" because of a personal preference. But when the change is sent to the trans-lator, she will have to consider, does that change the meaning? Does it alter the tense or subject of the sentence? Even if there is no difference in French and nothing needs to change, she's already spent thirty seconds deciding it's irrelevant. Multiply that by *all* the irrelevant changes (not to mention the consequential ones) and *all* the languages being translated, and you've created a costly, time-consuming change that could have been avoided.

We see it all the time with little things. If a URL is broken in English, it's going to be broken in every translation as well, so best make sure all your links work before you translate them into twenty languages. Recently, we worked with a company to translate a catalog of wines from Italian to English. We had worked with them before and had always translated the names of the wines into English as well. Their marketing department had recently decided that they wanted to keep all the product names in their original Italian. The problem is, no one told us of this change, and we didn't find out until we had already translated every wine name. It was a significant amount of work to go back and revert them all to their original Italian.

If these late-in-the-game changes are a persistent problem, it might behoove you to consider the method by which you create your materials. If legal or marketing are always swooping in at the last minute with time-consuming but essential changes, you might want to consider involving them earlier in the process.

FORMATTING

Imagine you are looking at a large food menu at a diner. There may be two columns on each page, and some photos in the mix. If you were to make that menu yourself in Microsoft Word, how would you line up those columns? Would you enter the text, and then hit the tab key until it all lines up nicely? How would you fit the photos, place them, and then type around them? You might be able to get away with that if you are printing it once in English and don't anticipate any changes. But if it is a document that is going to be translated into multiple languages, this can pose a serious problem. Different languages will require a different number of characters, and often a different alphabet, and you will immediately lose all of the formatting that you had intended.

This is a very simple example of what can be a recurring and complex problem—poorly formatted source material. Translation tools are designed to pull data from documents that are laid out properly, but if the source document isn't using the correct styles and rules, then each translation will have to be formatted individually. This means what could be properly formatted with the click of a button will now need to be manually formatted thirty times.

Generally, it's not a good idea to format a document to English unless you are a designer working in a design program. If you do have a designer working on a project, don't send an early, unformatted, or poorly formatted draft for translation, unless it is absolutely necessary for because of the size of the project. Sometimes we do have to start working on those early documents because of the amount of data. When this happens, we usually have to retranslate the well-formatted manual later on.

The general rule of thumb is this: send the material in its last possible format. For something that will be printed, it is usually in InDesign or another design program; for a website, it is the web pages or the CMS content driving the web site; and for an app, it will be the software resources. Whatever the case may be, the most economical way to proceed is to give us the material in its most advanced form.

SOFTWARE

Often translation software can be a great time-saving tool, but other times, it can cause problems. We will talk more about the benefits and pitfalls of using these kinds of tools later in the book in Misapplied Tools, but it is important to note how they can affect the materials presented to your translator.

Different content authors might be working in different locations, and this can affect their work. For example, if one programmer is located in England and one is located in America, there may be little spelling differences; they might spell the word "favorite" as "favourite." As a result, if a product uses the word "favorite" in their marketing ("Your favorite ice cream," for example), you might see it spelled differently in different documents.

To the average English reader, this might not matter, but when it passes through our translation software (which may have been used in yet *another* location) it might actually be translated differently. One spelling might translate to a word that means favorite, while the other might translate to a word that is closer to "preferred" or "beloved." This will mean the translator will have to go through and fix each reference manually for consistency.

This is one very specific example of how software might affect the documents provided for translation. If you have materials being supplied from different divisions, it is important to review for consistency *before* sending everything on to your translator.

PUTTING IN THE TIME UPFRONT

At times, what we are asking for might seem onerous. Sitting down with your engineering team, legal team, communications team, and marketing team in order to finalize materials might be a daunting prospect. It might be hard to convince certain team members that their aspect of the project is even relevant to translation (it's especially hard to convince software developers to take translation into account). However, the Brower Electronics debacle is just one example of how limited foresight can end up resulting in enormous costs and difficulties and can in fact put the entire project in jeopardy.

> Limited foresight can end up resulting in enormous costs and difficulties and can in fact put the entire project in jeopardy.

There are so many things to consider when you're prepping a document for translation, and having the whole team's input is essential. You want to anticipate certain questions that are sure to arise: How do the headers go with the body? What happens if you've got a typo below a graphic or the graphic is at the bottom of the page—does it pull the whole graphic onto the next page? What if the Spanish URL is longer than the English URL, and it shifts the column? What if you don't need the links to ingredients in certain countries—will you link to the American site? Figuring all of this out ahead of time is quite an upfront investment, but the more you get into the habit of doing it, the easier it will become.

We have seen this kind of commitment work with our long-term clients at AKIKO. These days, when they send us their materials, it takes us literally *minutes* to do the page layout for a language. They've done all of the work on their end, and we've built up a huge amount of institutional knowledge on ours. After all that, all we need to do is just push the button, and the savings for AKIKO are enormous.

6

MISAPPLIED TOOLS

SAN DIEGO, CALIFORNIA, 2013

The air in the office was still. Françoise and Ian waited. Jane, the chief content officer at Dallow-Klein, sighed as she turned the last page of the report. Ian shifted in his seat, and Françoise was lightly drumming her fingertips on the arm of her chair. Ian felt the urge to reach over and take her hand, but before he did, she looked up and they made eye contact. She smiled at him and put her hands in her lap. Jane sighed again and placed the report on her desk. It was a moment before she spoke.

"So, what you're saying is…" she started to say, then trailed off, as if distracted by something she saw in the hallway behind them. She had a habit of doing this—starting sentences but getting distracted by her own thoughts.

They waited for a moment for her to resume. After a moment, she did:

"Your final analysis is…" She trailed off again.

They waited another moment, then Françoise interjected, "Don't buy it."

"Don't buy it?"

"No."

Jane thought for a moment, then said, by way of clarification, "Don't buy it all?"

Françoise smiled at her. "Not at all."

"Well," she continued, "should we buy something else, then?"

"Not unless you want to throw away three hundred thousand dollars."

Jane leaned back in her chair and looked at Françoise. For the most part, their clients love her direct, no-nonsense approach, and Jane was no exception. This time, however, she seemed genuinely confused by this turn of events.

"The thing is, during the pilot, we made some discoveries," Ian said. "And in the end, we really think you can do without it."

Jane looked from one of them to the other. She was slight, with a casual, unhurried air about her. But having worked with her for a couple of years, the Hendersons knew she had a lot going on under the surface. She had overseen several projects that Rubric had managed, and pleased with their work, she had remained mostly hands off. They rarely had occasion to sit down in her office, conducting most of their oversight or postmortem meetings over lunch or drinks.

This project was a bit different. The company was considering a major purchase: a translation management system focused on their print catalogs. Ian and Françoise had encountered challenges when translating the catalogs and were familiar with the problems and inconsistencies the tool was meant to address. The CMS would be an enormous investment, so Jane wanted to get Ian and Françoise's opinion on it before they took the plunge.

Ian and Françoise had seen this scenario many times before. A company that is struggling to solve a problem meets a software vendor with a "perfect" solution. The pitch is smooth and promising, and the company is desperate for a quick fix. It's usually not until after the purchase is complete that it becomes clear this "perfect" solution is expensive, unwieldy, and not all it was cracked up to be.

But Dallow-Klein had Jane now, and she was thinking five, six steps ahead of the problem. She was wary of any simple solutions, so she asked Ian and Françoise to oversee a pilot project to test this new software before committing to buy. They were thrilled to be given this chance and took on the project.

They had spent a week in Milan working with the Dallow-Klein staff there, using the tool to extract information from the most recent English catalog to create a catalog in Italian. The company spared no expense for the pilot, and for everyone's travel, lodging, salary, and fees, they spent about $50,000 to do it right. They had made a significant investment and they were very anxious for it to go well. At first, they were impressed. The tool had a nice interface— it looked sleek and modern and had an application for use on all their devices. However, they quickly realized the rest of the tool was not as well crafted as the design. It could not handle large image files and kept freezing and crashing, leading to a very frustrating, unproductive experience.

During the process, they also came to understand where the internal, company-wide communication breakdowns were taking place. They got a clearer picture of what could be streamlined and how changes in the process could help clear up a lot of the confusion. After a week in Milan, the Hendersons determined Dallow-Klein probably didn't need this software at all. In their report, they outlined five concrete adjustments that could be made within the company to help address the same problems.

"So, after all of that…"

"It's not a tool you need," Françoise finished, this time not waiting to see if Jane would continue. "Not if you put these changes into place."

A moment of silence passed. Ian, usually a great judge of character, could not read Jane's expression. Was she angry that they had spent time and money on the pilot? Was she curious about what the fixes were? Was she bored and thinking about something else?

"I know you spent about fifty thousand dollars on the whole pilot project," Ian said carefully. "Are you disappointed?"

Jane looked up and finally smiled. "Disappointed?" She laughed. "I spent fifty thousand dollars, but saved two hundred and fifty thousand dollars. All in all, I'd say that's a pretty good deal."

TRANSLATION TOOLS

I have said before, translation is more of an art than a science. Because people fail to recognize translation as a content issue, they think they can "solve" the problems of translations with the right tool. While human expertise and oversight is always essential, the right tool can be a great asset to a project. But knowing which tool to buy, how to use it, and what it is made for is going to be very important to your translation journey.

> While human expertise and oversight is always essential, the right tool can be a great asset to a project.

Quite often companies are interested in buying their own translation software for internal use. For multibillion-dollar global companies this might make sense. However, for the most part, companies do not have the budget or content volume to warrant this kind of tool.

Aside from the issue of size, most companies do not anticipate the larger picture of translation when they buy their own translation tools. For one thing, if translating content was as simple as buying a translation tool, everyone would do it. But despite what many salespeople will tell you, the purchase of said tool is only the first step. In fact, manufacturers don't even necessarily see a profit from the sale of the tool itself. The real profits start to roll in on the other side of the sale, when they begin to sell training packages and upgrades. This is often not made clear to buyers until it is too late. Most translation tools require intense training in order to be useful, and this can be a major strain on internal staff.

The other misdirection a salesperson might employ is to tell you that if you use their tool, you will save 70 percent of your translation cost. This is extremely misleading, because it relies on the premise that translators are not already using tools and passing the savings on to clients. This is not true for the most part, and certainly not in our case.

When it comes to translation tools, there is a huge difference between a machine translation tool, something similar to Google Translate, and a computer-aided translation tool. The former is fine in some situations. The latter is meant to accompany professionals in content translation by pooling information and making translations based on previously stored content. We are using all the of the best tools and passing those time savings on to our customer.

I understand the impetus for a company to purchase in-house translation software. Those tools end up storing years of important, crucial, time-saving data, and it's the kind of intellectual property executives want to protect and have access to at all times. Because most translators are contractors who often work off-site, retaining that information can prove challenging if you are not working with the right translators.

When we came on board with Brower Electronics for example, they had been working with a translator who was always late. In addition to that, they were not sharing their amassed database of translations with the Brower team, which meant it was difficult for Brower to part ways with them—ostensibly, they were being held hostage (not unlike the relationship between Q Translations and AKIKO when we first came on board). The translators were not even taking the time to update their own database consistently, and so changes and updates were not being recorded, and the same mistakes were being repeated over and over again.

In this situation, it would be tempting for Brower to invest in their own translation tool to prevent being left out in the cold. Instead, they hired us. Because of our fastidiousness in terms of building institutional knowledge with our clients, and our guiding principle to never leave a client without all their information, they didn't need to buy their own translation tool. This saved them countless hours, hundreds of thousands of dollars, and a great deal of frustration.

CONNECTORS

Another big category of tools we see is what is called "API connectors." Without getting too technical, connectors help to transfer data among different components, allowing us to pull information for translation from a website, for example. Given the complicated and technical nature of some of this work, having the right connectors can be invaluable. It's a tool that we offer to people within our service, and one that makes our jobs imminently more manageable.

However, as important as they are, connectors cannot do it all. There is still work to be done to structure and polish the information so that it can be manipulated. We recently worked with a travel agency who were courting an international audience and wanted to translate their website. They had built their own database, so we had to create a connector in order to extract all the information we needed. The technical details of this particular project are not important. What matters is, in the end, the connector did about 80 percent of the job, and we handled the last 20 percent manually. Getting the data out of the website did not prove to be the most difficult part, but more the fact that data on the website was not structured or organized in a disciplined way.

For example, they might have a post about a sale they were running, and one person tagged it as "a special deal." Later, someone else changed the tag to "monthly special." When they were trying to push it on a particular day, they might go in again and tag it as "Special of the day."

Because of the inconsistencies in the way the information was being entered, the connector could only go so far to interpret this information; it ended up requiring a human touch. We worked with the client to streamline their offers so that the content would be easier to pull in the future. The tool was extremely important to the success of this project, but even so, a tool can only take you so far.

Another client brought us on to translate their website into six languages. It was a small site, only about twenty pages, and they wanted to develop a tool to help get the content out of the website and back in—a connector.

Knowing the cost, training, and consistency required to make a tool worth this kind of development, we advised them not to bother—for twenty pages and six languages, it was much easier and cost effective to just to pull out and reenter the information manually.

It is tempting to try to find a tool that will make the process more technical and repeatable, and had it been a website with a 150 pages, going into thirty-five different languages, it would make sense to develop such a program. But despite the appeal of such connectors, it will not magically do the work; we can tell you that from experience. You will always need professionals to go the extra distance, to close the gap between where the tool's capabilities end, and the job is finished.

CONTENT MANAGEMENT SYSTEMS

When it comes to operating tools, the biggest price tag items are the content management systems (CMS) or product information management (PIM) tools. These tend to be large, overarching programs used for websites, marketing materials, technical documentation, or software. They are very large investments, so the hope is they will be effective, efficient tools. There are many salespeople who will be happy to sell you their version of this catchall tool, but we urge our clients to confer with us before they commit to any purchase.

When you are dealing with a multinational corporation, it's important to remember that you will not be inputting *one* set of data into your CMS or PIM—it's going to be ten, twenty, or even thirty different sets, because each language is its own set of data. If a vendor just says, "Oh yes, don't worry. We can write a bit of French on this," it's likely they are not fully grasping the extent of the need.

Another thing to consider is how much a tool will realistically be used. Many of our clients employ diverse types of content, and it may not make sense to have all the content flow through one CMS tool. Again, this is not how the salesperson will frame it initially. That's not to say a vendor is intentionally lying if she says, "This tool can handle *everything*," it's very likely a powerful tool with a wide range of capabilities. But she might not be taking into account the overhead required to make the tool work, to adapt it to the diversity of content, or to handle the multiple sets of data that comes with multiple translations.

A problem we see quite often is that clients buy a large CMS tool to solve an English problem, because their first operating language is English. They lose sight of the fact that they're operating internationally and need to think multidimensionally.

We saw this concern in action during our early

days working with Destinations Worldwide. When first implementing a CMS with a vendor, they asked about the multiple languages it would need to handle. They were told it would be able to function in all the languages, but they needed to sort it out for the English first. They worked for a couple of years on the English, and then when it finally came to the translations, the CMS couldn't fully support the translation workflow. The two years ended up being completely wasted effort.

We recognize that choosing a CMS or PIM is already a complicated business, and we're asking you to consider yet another very important aspect of data, but it will be important.

Imagine you are developing a program for air traffic control. It would be a very simple job if the plan was based on a hundred airplanes taking off in the morning, and then the same hundred airplanes coming back at the end of the day. But air traffic control deals with *thousands* of airplanes taking off and landing from different airports around the world, at all times of day and night. They are different sizes, fly at different speeds, carry a different number of people, and have different distances to travel. Dealing with the airplanes that take off and land in an airport requires a very sophisticated management—so does your international company. A program that only deals with the English data is merely doing a fraction of the work.

My best advice—in addition to bringing your translation team to consult on choosing your tools—is to run a pilot project first, the same way Dallow-Klein did. At the end of the day, they spent fifty thousand dollars to find out it was a tool they didn't need. While fifty thousand dollars is not an insignificant amount of money, compared to the three hundred thousand dollars they would have spent on the tool, not to mention the training, upgrades, and fixes, it was worth it for the amount they saved.

POOR USER JOURNEYS

BUENOS AIRES, ARGENTINA, 2019

Ian checked his phone again to make sure he was still on hold. He was surprised that a ticket agency that handled so many music events didn't have any waiting music on the phone line. Especially since it seemed they had no qualms about keeping a customer waiting for what was going on seven minutes.

"But how would they choose what to play?" he wondered aloud to himself. As a ticket agency, they handled heavy metal concerts, live rock bands, singer-songwriters, lavish musicals, and operas. He was calling to buy tickets for the last and would have probably been nonplussed if he had been forced to listen to some heavy metal music while waiting. Then again, silence was unnerving. He looked at his phone again. Eight minutes.

He sighed. Françoise's birthday was five weeks away and what she wanted most was to see *La Bohème* at the Teatro Colón. They had arrived in Buenos Aires late last night, but would only be at the hotel for one day before venturing on to a more rural area for three weeks. Phone and internet service would be unreliable there, and he knew the opera would sell out very quickly, so he needed to secure tickets today in order to make sure he would have them for her birthday.

If he could pull off this unexpected gift, he knew Françoise would be ecstatic, and maybe even a little impressed. After all these years, it was still a thrill to see that look in her eye, the one that said, "You can still surprise me, after all."

He had snuck out of their room to try to make the call in secret. It wasn't that the idea had struck him. In fact, he had already been trying to arrange tickets for two weeks. The Teatro Colón had a gorgeous website that had been translated (and translated well, Ian was quick to notice), and he had no trouble identifying the show and the dates he was looking for.

The problem was, they had outsourced their ticket sales to a ticket agency, and their website was strictly in Spanish. Françoise was the multilinguist of the family, and Ian struggled to understand what he was looking for. He briefly considered downloading what he could see and using their translation tools, but there was no chance he could do that without Françoise noticing. Calling the number provided had also proven difficult because of the time difference. He realized a few days ago that if he was going to pull off this surprise, it was going to have to wait until he was in the country and could call directly.

He was getting ready to hum to himself for his own amusement when someone finally picked up on the other end.

"Buenos días, en qué puedo ayudarle?" said the friendly voice on the other end of the line.

"Buenos días, habla inglés?" Ian asked.

"Yes, sir, how can I help you?"

"Phew," Ian thought, feeling like he had finally caught a break. This should be easy from here on in.

"I'd like two tickets to the opera at Teatro Colón please. What are the best seats you have available?" Ian was feeling excited now. Imagine if he could surprise Françoise with really spectacular seats.

"For which show, señor?"

"For *La Bohème*," he said.

"That opera doesn't open for five weeks," said the voice on the line.

"Yes, I know."

"Tickets for all operas at the Teatro Colón only go on sale thirty days in advance," said the voice, sounding distracted and maybe even a little bored.

Ian's heart sank to his stomach. "Thirty days in advance! So, I can't buy tickets for another five days?"

"That's right."

"I won't be able to do that," Ian said, getting very annoyed. "I'll be out of range to make the call for three weeks."

"You can call back in three weeks," said the voice.

"Will there be tickets left at that point?"

"Probably not."

Ian was losing his patience. "I've been on hold for ten minutes. Why isn't this rule made clear?"

"The policy is clearly stated on our website, señor."

This might have been true. Ian had no reason to doubt it. But of course, he had been unable to read the website.

He was so disappointed, for a moment he couldn't speak.

"Señor? Are you there?"

"Yes, I'm here. Is there nothing that can be done to get the tickets now?"

"No, I'm sorry. Would you like to get tickets for *Tristan und Isolde*? That's on next week."

"No, I certainly would not," said Ian, his annoyance apparent in his voice. "No offense to Wagner, but Françoise's birthday is not next week. Besides, we won't even be here." He realized this person on the phone had no idea what he was taking about.

"Thank you for your time." He promptly hung up.

This was the kind of thing that he and Françoise were always warning their clients about. If they are not aware of who their customers are and what their needs might be, they will lose business. Ian was willing to bet that a large portion of the patrons attending the Teatro Colón were from English-speaking countries. So many questions ran through his mind as he stood outside on the hotel grounds.

How many customers ended up frustrated and annoyed because they were confused by the policy?

How much would the cost of translating the ticket website be, compared to how much more they would bring in through sales?

Why not at least put a notice that tickets need to be purchased ahead of time in English on the website?

What was he going to get Françoise for her birthday?

That thought broke his reverie. He knew Françoise would appreciate the anecdote as an illustration of a poor user journey, but it would not replace tickets to the opera as a gift.

He approached the concierge at the desk. The young man smiled brightly at him. He looked trustworthy enough. Besides, at this point, Ian had no choice. He took a wad of cash from his pocket and placed it on desk.

"If I give you very clear instructions, can you do me a favor in about five days?"

POOR USER JOURNEYS

The experience of your customers is paramount to your success as a business. This might sound intuitive, but it's actually easy to lose sight of this concept when you are creating and marketing a product. There will be moments throughout the process

> **The experience of your customers is paramount to your success as a business.**

when different things feel most important, whether it is having the sleekest, most state-of-the-art product;

finding the most eye-catching advertising; or hitting the market before anyone else. All of these things are essential to surviving and standing out in a crowded market. But the user journey you create for your customers when buying your product should be the first thing you consider when developing your strategy.

Throughout this book, we advocated for every company to employ a chief content officer to oversee all content in every language, and this position would help quell problems that often arise around user journeys. However, even without that officer in place, there are steps that can be taken to ensure that your company is doing everything to maximize the experience of your customer.

AWARENESS

Awareness of your customer is the first and most basic step toward improving their experience. If you are planning on taking your product global, you have to be aware of how it will be perceived, purchased, and used in other countries. This can be more challenging than expected. Many products designed for and by Americans are in high demand in other countries, but it doesn't mean that the user experience will be exactly the same.

Consider the experience of getting from an airport to your hotel. I always chance it—I get off my plane and queue up in the taxi line. Many people prefer public transit; others will prebook a car on an app or through a service. Ultimately, we are all going on the same journey of getting from the airport to our hotel, but the paths we take are all unique.

Customers for your product are like this as well. If you are selling a vacuum cleaner, there are endless pathways by which people are going to land on your product. Some of them are finding it through word of mouth, others through advertising; still others might have read about it in an article. They are going to buy it in all different ways, too. Some will purchase it in a retail store, while others will order it online. The impetus to buy will vary as well. Some might be searching for cleaning products in general, and some will be searching for vacuum cleaners specifically, while loyal customers who have bought and loved your brand before might just be looking for your newest product.

All of this is as unique as the individual personalities of your customer, but many things can be predicted by the trends and customs of certain geographical locations. When you are marketing your American-designed product in Japan, you must consider what the average Japanese person is looking for and how that might differ from your American audience.

It is best to build your awareness before you even start developing your marketing plan—even in the US. So much of the marshy ground could be avoided if there was a moment early in the process when the American, South American, and Asian teams all got together and said, "Here's what we're thinking of doing. How will this work in Peru? How will it work in Osaka? What are we not anticipating? How will it *translate*?"

Of course, we know why this doesn't often happen. Everyone is under enormous pressure to get the product finished, manufactured, marketed, and distributed by a rapidly approaching deadline. Stopping to consider the average buyer in Jakarta does not feel like a priority. We understand this is difficult, and it can't happen overnight. That's why we have developed these steps toward improving the user journey that can be employed to different degrees at any point in any company. And in the meantime, you are developing awareness within your own company on different levels, and eventually it will become part of the company's DNA.

IDENTIFYING PERSONAS

Identifying the personas that make up your clientele is as important as identifying what your product is and what it does. It is not enough to know *what* you are selling, you must understand *to whom* you are selling. These customers, or "personas," may differ from country to country for a variety of reasons.

Our client Brisk is a very good example of how the target market can shift from region to region. Brisk manufactures cleaning technology equipment, and in the United States, their products retail in the middle/upper range. However, in India, Brisk's products are at the top end of the luxury market. This significantly changes the way the products are marketed, where they are sold, and how the content is communicated.

For a client like Brisk, in the early stages of a new product, they have to identify what the market looks like from country to country, then divide them into segments. For example, the market for the washers is very different from the market for vacuum cleaners. And within the vacuum cleaner segment, some of the customers are industrial users, and others are households. Among industrial users, the competition is other very high-end, specialist industrial manufacturers. Among young household users, the competition is the makers of colorful, trendy vacuum robots.

All of this requires careful calculation and planning, and unless marketing and production are aware of the different personas, they can't tailor the product or advertising correctly. Different features will attract each of these target markets as they shop in different places. There are additional variables when expanding into international markets, and the more carefully you consider your customers, the more thoughtful and effective your marketing will be.

> **The more carefully you consider your customers, the more thoughtful and effective your marketing will be.**

Another thing that is important to consider when identifying personas is that the location where your customer originates is not always the same location where they are using your product. For example, if someone is using a restaurant app to look up restaurants in Seoul, it doesn't mean that they are in Korea, or need the script to be in Korean. It could be Koreans looking to book a restaurant, or it could be Americans traveling in Korea. It could be Koreans living abroad, checking to see if they can book when they are next in Korea. Identifying multiple personas and anticipating their paths will limit the frustration your customers encounter and will improve their user experience.

It makes sense for executives to know who is buying their product and lean on that information when planning their translations, yet we rarely see that effort being made. Too often the focus is instead on getting the lowest possible cost of translation. Instead of recognizing translation as a tool for maximizing profits, they consider it more of an extra international tax.

GROUND RULES

When planning the experience your users will have, it's important to develop clear practices that are universal throughout your company. We call these the "ground rules," and they are the brand identifiers or experiential constants that you want every customer to recognize when they are dealing with your product.

Imagine that famous fast food restaurant you probably passed on the way to work today. What is the symbol that comes to mind? Picture yourself walking into a famous coffee shop chain. What kind of service do you expect to receive? Consider the phone you use every day. What design elements can you take for granted will be in place? Chances are, no matter what city or country of the world you are in, these basic, identifying factors will be the same.

These are a corporation's ground rules—the content that will never change no matter the region. The ground rules often include a logo or signature color. It can be values of customer service, or user-friendly features. Whatever your ground rules are, they are the elements that make your company unique, that create its identity. Without the ground rules in place, your company is not your company.

However, not everything can be a hard and fast rule, and it is important to be flexible when bringing your product to foreign markets. Translating is about communicating overall content, and if something is too US centric, you can lose your international audience in confusion or annoyance. If you overextend the ground rules, and make everything about your English marketing strategy ironclad, it can backfire.

For example, when the marketing gets into the hands of your Spanish team, they might look at it and say, "This doesn't speak to our demographic here in Spain. We need to redo all of it." If they feel that you haven't considered their region in any way, they might assume that none of the branding was created with their audience in mind, and they might scrap it all. Then you are at risk of losing your look, your values, and the very essence of what makes your company, your company.

LOCALIZATION AND SPECIFICATION

After you have established what your bottom-line ground rules are, you need to be ready to get local and specific with your strategy. You've identified the personas to whom you are selling, and you've established what will remain consistent from country to country. Now it is time to dig into the culture of the region and figure out how to use the local information to sell to your identified market. If you are targeting DJs in Singapore with your headphones, where are they getting their product recommendations? If you are selling coffee to hipsters in Denmark, will Facebook be effective, or do you need to tap into the world of Instagram influencers? All of these details will vary from country to country and should be taken into account when planning your translations, then carefully communicated to your translators.

Another important consideration is how your advertising will work. If you are used to online ads, but you're now working in a country that relies heavily on billboards, the amount of text you are going to be able to use will be limited. Can you express in eight to ten words what you've been saying in forty in English? Conversely, how does the primary logo you've chosen work if you are going from a billboard to an online ad?

Will it still be clear what the image is? Will it evoke the same emotional response on a smaller platform?

A company or product tagline can be a very tricky thing to translate. In America, a tagline might be essential to a company's branding. The instinct is to make it a ground rule. But a tagline almost always requires much more than a straight translation. We don't always realize it, but a tagline often calls on cultural touchstones, or prior collective knowledge that we take for granted. Even linguistically, a tagline might rely on language peculiarities that are not universal from culture to culture.

Imagine you're working at a popular travel company that helps people book flights, hotels, and car rentals all over the world. Your tagline for your American clientele is "We're willing to go there." It's clever, because "go there" is a popular American expression for going "out of bounds," or pushing the envelope on what you'll talk about or explore. It also works on a literal level because it conjures images of traveling off the beaten path, and forward motion— literally *going*. A tagline that works on multiple levels shows a sophisticated marketing strategy.

However, this phrase might not translate very well to French, or Hebrew, or Finnish, where the cultural references are different, and there is no direct translation for this phrase. Insisting on this tagline as a ground rule, not allowing for localization and specification could result in a poor translation, like something that essentially means "Eager to travel there," or "Ready to make our way to that place," or some other uninspired, meaningless phrase. Finding a translation with the equivalent level of irreverent, succinct cleverness might mean changing the sentiment a bit, but a slightly different phrase that captures the spirit of your English tagline will do more to further your brand.

Flexibility is important when considering your user. The people and the products they buy will vary from country to country, and your marketing and process will need to do the same. It can't stay too uniform because it won't speak to all the audiences, but it can't be too individualized because then you lose your brand identity. Creating a balance between preserving the global brand and serving the local needs will ensure a positive user journey for your customer.

INSPIRATIONAL OUTLOOK

EDINBURGH, SCOTLAND, 2006

"Ian! Ian! Wake up!"

Ian's eyes flew open at the sound of his name being frantically called. Françoise was standing over him. Her eyes were bright despite the darkness of the room, and she was shaking him awake.

"What is it? What's wrong? Is the house on fire?"

"No, no, nothing like that," she said dismissively. "It's good news. Meet me in the office."

She flicked on the lamp next to the bed, then turned on her heels and walked briskly out the door, leaving Ian confused in a half-dream state. He looked at the clock. Two in the morning. He rubbed his eyes and yawned. This had better be good.

A few moments later with his robe and a glass of water, he found Françoise standing over her desk, looking quite pleased with herself, he thought. Her desk was always organized, a symbol of her fast-working, efficient mind. At the moment, it was supporting several stacks of papers, which Ian knew to be CSA Research papers they had recently sought out.

"OK. What's this all about?"

"I found it."

"Found what?"

"Exactly what we were looking for."

He noticed then that she was holding sheet of paper in her hands. Actually, she was clutching it to her chest, like a person might their favorite first-edition book. Ian was suddenly interested and sat in the comfortable armchair opposite the desk.

"I'm listening."

It had been several weeks since they had embarked on a restrategizing mission for Rubric. The business was successful and had been for the last decade or so. Their philosophy of translation was sound and serving their clients well. But they wanted to go bigger. They were looking for a way to reach a wider audience, to help more companies embark on the journey of globalization or improve the path they were already on. They were looking for a new strategy, a new method to redirect their own journey, and they were looking into the industry research for inspiration.

CSA Research was a leader in global market research and translation services. They had been working with CSA for years, and since embarking on their new strategic planning, they had been poring through papers and articles they thought might be helpful. The office was full of such papers, and they had been reading for days.

At around eleven o'clock the previous evening, Ian, his eyes bleary and brain muddled, had gone to bed, assuming Françoise would follow him shortly. He was wrong. Françoise had stayed up and continued reading, and as she was now explaining to him, she had hit upon something. Something big.

"It's all in here," she was saying excitedly, tapping the page in her hand. "CSA developed it, and there's a full report, sixty-two pages. I've downloaded it already. I'll print you your own copy; I'd rather not share. We'll each want to take our own notes. But I can tell from the preview that it's exactly what we're looking for. It's going to be perfect."

"That's great, Françoise," Ian said, trying to keep up. "But why? What is it?"

She smiled her brilliant smile. "That's the thing; it's everything we're already doing. It's everything we've always done, by instinct. But here, they've written it down, quantified it, systemized it."

She handed him the paper. It was already covered in her notes. As he began to skim it, he saw immediately what had her so excited, what had her wake him in the middle of the night.

"It's like they've articulated what we've been trying to say all this time."

"Exactly! And they've developed a framework to put it all in place, something that simplifies the process into steps that can be adjusted for each client," Françoise was pacing now.

"This is really exciting," Ian said, still waking up to the idea.

"I know! And the best part is, it comes naturally to us. We're already doing it. We've just been self-taught. Now we will have the understanding of how to teach it to others." She snatched the pages back from him to look over them again. She considered what she was looking at carefully.

"Ian," she said, suddenly thoughtful, "I feel

like this will really give people hope. A systemized, organized approach to our philosophy will help people understand that what we're saying can really be implemented. They can measure it and see concrete results. It's going to help us reach more people, grow Rubric, bring our ideas to more of the world."

"I'm with you, a hundred percent," said Ian. "But you've got a bit of a head start, as usual, and I was in a deep sleep just moments ago. I have some questions."

"Sorry, love, I'm just so excited. What is it you want to know?

"Well, for starters, what's it called?"

Françoise laughed. "Oh, just that?" She put the pages down in front of her. "It's called the Localization Maturity Model—LMM for short. And it's going to change everything, by hardly changing a thing."

LOCALIZATION MATURITY MODEL

When we discovered the Localization Maturity Model (LMM) while journeying on our own path of self-improvement, it really was as though a light bulb went on above our collective heads. Here was a well-defined articulation of what we had always done instinctually at Rubric, with the added benefit of a clear and proven framework.

Up until our discovery of the LMM, it was not always easy to measure our clients' and our own improvement. We knew things were getting better when they implemented our philosophies, but we didn't always have a reference point from which to gauge where they had started and where they had arrived. The metrics measurement of the LMM puts stakes in the ground in a number of different areas and helps us say, "This is where we are today. Now let's plan for where we want to be in the future."

In an early meeting with one of our clients who develops specialized software for shipping companies, they expressed interest in extending their work into a number of new languages. They had one of their developers working on it, and he proudly stated that he had optimized the solution and could now update one language in less than a day, when everything else was in place. If they hired four or five more developers to work on it, they could be working in eight to ten languages by the end of the year.

Because of our experience, we knew that there are companies out there who are integrating ten times the amount of volume in forty languages, and it was taking them ten minutes. When we told him that, it was a blow to the developer's ego, for a moment. But when he really leaned in to listen to what we were saying, he started to understand there were things he could be doing to make his life easier and the product more efficient. The first thing that we identified was that they should work with more automation and see how it could change their output.

In the end, we made great strides for them, because by implementing the LMM, setting clear goals, and taking concrete metrics, we were able to develop a framework for how they can improve and reduce the work of one day to one hour.

SO HOW DOES IT WORK?

As you can tell by now, we are excited about the LMM. We were thrilled when we found it in 2006, and we continue to extol its efficacy and introduce it to our clients today. However, the LMM is not a magic wand—it is not something to throw at a problem that will solve all woes. It is not even a formula that you can apply and follow by the numbers. There is no easy fix to the problems outlined in this book, and every company, with its specific challenges and idiosyncrasies, will have to find its own path.

But here's the good news: the LMM is a framework, which means it can be applied broadly and adjusted accordingly. And here's the even better news: *it works*. Because it is not a one-size-fits-all solution, each company can apply this framework to their individual needs and to individual problems. If you follow the framework, you will see improvement.

> **Each company can apply this framework to their individual needs and to individual problems. If you follow the framework, you will see improvement.**

As we describe the steps, you will see that they are all very intertwined, and it is hard to identify exactly the order they come in. The order we lay out here is generally the order in which the LMM is applied, but the success of the framework is dependent on all the steps working together simultaneously.

1. GOVERNANCE

Governance is arguably the most important aspect of the LMM. Getting a funding model in place and clarifying what sponsors can expect will affect everything that follows. Once you know what the budget is, you can work out what can be done for that amount of money.

This is where governance comes in. If your goal

is to expand your market into ten more languages, you have to make a plan and identify the steps: by what date do you want to have implemented those ten languages? What do you *mean* by ten languages? Are you going to translate *everything* into ten languages? Identifying the metrics and having the means by which to track them is essential.

When we began working with Destinations, their team was working on lining up the Android and iOS applications in the same languages. However, the Android had its platform in sixty languages, while the iOS only existed in forty-eight, so the process that dictated they should translate all the same languages for both platforms created a lot of waste.

For example, Android can support Galician, but iOS cannot. Despite this, the developers coded it for both, because that is just their policy.

When we discovered this in a meeting, we asked, "What are you doing with the Galician and other eleven languages you developed for the iOS platform, even though it is not supported?"

The VP turned to the product lead and said, "Yes, why do we do that?"

There was no real answer except that is the process that had been laid out. They had a tool driving the process, which was in turn driving the strategy. They had it all backward. When we began implementing the LMM, it gave us an opportunity to meet with more senior managers, and we explained that it was their role of governance that would ensure that the tools were in sync with the process.

Measuring success is essential to the success of the framework, and is an important part of governance. You must know where you are starting and gauge your progress as you go. The metrics might be the most important part of the process. The LMM gives us a more formal approach for collecting key performance indicators and allows us to clearly see where there are improvements. This also applies to growth goals, helping us put processes in place that will hasten arrival at those goals, rather than just putting a dream out into the world and hoping it happens.

We had been working with Brisk for a few years when they asked us to track how long it took us to get purchase orders from the finance department. They were under strict instructions that their suppliers were not allowed to start work before a purchase order had been issued, but the finance department was taking so long that in order for us to meet deadlines, we had to "cheat." Once we collected the metrics of when we actually started work, compared to when we got the official go-ahead from finance, our partners took that information to the finance department. "As you can see," they said, "if we followed your advice, we would never deliver on time." Because of this, the finance staff instantly realized that this was not a sustainable way of doing things and adjusted their process accordingly.

This billing method had been the accepted practice for years, but it wasn't working well for anyone—neither the clients nor the finance department, who were constantly being defied and ignored. Just by tracking the metric and presenting them the data, everyone had a better handle on how the goal could be achieved and adjusted their process accordingly.

Clearly, this example is not even related to translation, but the LMM can be applied in numerous ways, and in this case, we were merely a good measurement of how their interdepartmental contracting was functioning. That's the whole point of the LMM. It's not a question of nickel-and-diming the translation. It's about a holistic approach to what the organization needs to do to improve.

Part of implementing the LMM is providing a company with the scorecard. We come into a company, do an assessment of their functions, and give them a score from -3 to +5. On the negative side people are deliberately undermining efforts to start translating. Level 0 is when companies just ignore the need to translate. We tend to deal with companies who are between +1 and +4, as +5 is pretty much unheard of.

The scorecard is based on some fairly objective metrics. We ask about sixty simple questions about how the company is run. "Do you have a strategy, or don't you have a strategy?" Or, "Do you have a person dedicated to language, yes, no?" The questions are grouped into the five areas of the LMM: Governance, Strategy, Process, Organization, and Automation. Each "yes" will get one point and each "no" zero points. We add up the number and work out a grade for each section, before calculating the overall score. At the end of the survey, your average is your score. It gives us an overall metric of how healthy your company, division or team is in terms of Localization maturity, and which areas need more attention.

Gathering this information and informing executives of their score not only gives us a metric from which we can drop a goal post, but it can also serve as quite a motivating factor. We have seen that score inspire people to improve, seek help, and identify areas for improvement, all so they can move up this scale toward the magical "level five."

2. STRATEGIZING FOR THE GOAL

A large company-wide goal might be what you are aiming for initially, something like "entering the European market." But the LMM encourages you to clarify and specify that goal, with concrete objectives and milestones that can be measured with metrics. A more specific goal would be, "We want to increase sales by $50 million in that region, which means we can spend $100,000 on translations." It still brings you toward the larger goal of entering the European market, but it also involves a clear strategy on how you're going to do that, with a clear and measurable goal, while being focused on revenue rather than expenditure.

When you know what your goal is, you can strategize around the bottom line. Maybe your goal is to cut your translation costs by 50 percent. We can solve that immediately by just doing half the work. But that isn't much of a strategy, and it's not going to tie in with your business objectives, which is to grow sales. So, in that case we develop a strategy by considering where the money is being spent at the moment. You might be overspending in markets that are flat or consistent enough that you can reinvest elsewhere. You can trim costs by examining where the new growth opportunities are and shifting your resources. Again, it's not an expenditure problem, but a question of where you want your business to go, where the new frontier lies.

3. PROCESS

Now that you have your governance and goals in place, you can observe and adjust how your process is working. This will be unique to each company, department, and problem that you are tackling.

When the Brisk finance department realized that the process they had in place seemed good on paper but was totally dysfunctional in practice, they set about creating a new process. Now, every time a new project comes in they open a purchase order with a limit of $100,000. And then whenever there is a new project, it is put against that pre-approved purchase order. Once that purchase order runs out, a new one is created.

This new process was completely different from the one they had in place for years. It was also more efficient, more detailed, more responsive to the company's needs, and saved time and manpower.

This new process, created in response to the goal and metrics identified by the LMM, was specific to Brisk, their capacity, and their needs. Another company might not have the flexibility to open a

$100,000 purchase order or might have some other legal requirements to take into consideration. The process by which you address your goals will be as unique as your company, which is why the LMM does not purport to be a recipe you must follow to the letter, but a series of guiding principles that will help create a smoother process.

4. ORGANIZATION

Organization means having center of excellence for global content. It's one thing to make a plan, but people are at the heart of your company, and they are the ones who have to execute it effectively. Having a person who is calling the shots, keeping an eye on the big picture, and making sure people are meeting their metrics is the key to success.

> Having a person who is calling the shots, keeping an eye on the big picture, and making sure people are meeting their metrics is the key to success.

Often when a new strategic plan is created, there is a need to hire new staff, either internal or contractors. It is not enough to identify the need for new staff—their roles within the company must be carefully outlined. What is the scope of their work? Is it only related to the new objectives, or are they folded into the larger company? Often new employees are brought on to work to a dedicated project and end up being siloed. Isolation from the rest of the company can lead to mistakes and confusion, as we explained in an earlier chapter.

A huge part of organization is also clear oversight. If new staff is designated to these newly identified goals, who is overseeing them? Whether they answer to someone in middle management in the finance department, or a C-level executive will make a big difference in terms of how they perceive their role, and how everyone else in the company perceives them.

We advocate throughout this book for companies to hire a chief content officer to oversee all global content and to simply "bang heads together," making sure everyone is communicating and doing their jobs. This is a big commitment, and companies are not always ready to pull the trigger. However, a new strategic goal often requires *someone* to be in charge of the new direction.

The instinct might be to promote someone lower in the hierarchy to do this, both to advance from within and to minimize the cost. When you do this, you send a signal to everyone else about the importance and scale of the project. If you do not put your best in charge, you cannot expect the best work to emerge. If you want everyone to take this new direction seriously, it helps to put someone higher up in charge. At the very least, you can pair your newly promoted employee with an executive who can throw their weight around when necessary.

5. AUTOMATION

The fifth and final pillar is automation. We find that a lot of prospects know they have a problem with translation, and so they try to jump right to this step. They go out, they buy a tool, and they hope the tool will fix the problem. We talked a lot about this in chapter 6, and as we stated there, there is no dearth of vendors who will be happy to sell you a "quick-fix" to your problem. More often than not, it is a colossal waste of time and manpower, because the tools will only work if you've got the other four LMM pillars in place first.

That said, buying the right tools and knowing how to use them can be of great help when you have good governance, strategy, firm processes, and a functioning organization. Automation will help you cut down on the human labor involved, and that will save you money.

We were thrilled when we found LMM, and we are enthusiastic about sharing it with our clients. On our journey, it has served as an important vehicle toward our destination. We believe that tools like the LMM can inspire and motivate companies and will provide hope that when things are difficult, they can indeed be improved.

AFTERWORD

In this book's introduction, we spoke of translation as a journey. It might seem like a romantic idea for a business necessity, but in our experience, it is accurate. Our passion for communication and connection runs deep, and our excitement about solving problems and working out complexities is at the core of our business ethic. We believe that every business, every product, and every project has unique needs and its own path to success in a global market.

Since we began Rubric in 1994, we have seen companies succeed by employing our philosophies and practices when it comes to global content. AKIKO is just one shining example of a company whose executives and department members understood our idea for global content, and they were willing to go on a journey with us. Because of that willingness, we learned many important lessons together. And throughout the course of our business relationship, they expanded into a billion-dollar company on the international market.

We wanted to write this book in order to document the experiences along the way that have made us smarter, more efficient, more agile, and more attuned to the needs and trends of the industry. Many of these experiences were also profound learning moments. Many made us laugh along the way.

Now that we have reached the end of this book, we wanted to leave you with a few parting thoughts that you might take with you into your next international endeavor:

Remember that content is a revenue driver. Too often translating content is seen merely as an expense. In reality, when you are paying it the careful attention it deserves—preparing your content in consultation with your whole team and taking into consideration the needs of your brand and the culture of your customers—the right content will make much more money than it will cost.

Raise the profile of global content within your company. In general, people don't have a good understanding of how important global content is, or how much work goes into getting it right. When your executives and team members start to comprehend the importance and value of good global content, it will begin to shift attitudes toward translation.

Finally, and perhaps most importantly, **this is doable.** Changing attitudes, perceptions, and behavior is not always easy, and it may take time, but it is far from an impossible dream. We have done it and seen it done many times over, and once you get the right elements in place, it might happen a lot faster than you think. Some journeys take time, and others move quickly, but if you know your destination, it is always worth taking the leap.

The truth is, the journey is never truly complete, because by the time you've reached your original destination, you've most likely identified a new goal—a higher height to climb, a further distance to run. There is satisfaction at reaching the end of the path, but also excitement about what the next leg of the adventure will bring.

When it comes to translating your content for a global audience, the method of travel is up to you. You can begin digging a tunnel every time you start anew. Or you can take the benefit of lessons learned, apply these time-tested concepts, and hop onto the smooth, untroubled freeway toward your destination. We believe that applying the concept of translation as a content issue will allow you to do the latter, and that will yield a much more worry-free, cost-effective way of reaching a global audience.

Thank you for taking this journey with us.

ACKNOWLEDGMENTS

I would like to thank Advantage for helping publish this book. Firstly, Elaine Best for keeping me on track with the many tasks required to get the book completed. David Lott, for shaping my random thoughts into something coherent, Alix Sobler for her assistance in getting these thoughts captured, Josh Houston for making sure nothing was missed, and Carly Blake for creating the cover on the first attempt.

To Susannah Eccles, who has been with us for most of the journey and is now leading the Quest. Rebecca Metcalf for working out what we need during the Quest, as well as the rest of the wonderful Rubric staff present and past, each of whom contributed something unique for our journey. To our clients who have given us reason for our Quest, and all our suppliers who make it happen.

Finally, my deepest gratitude goes to my Fellow Business Founder, Françoise Henderson for joining me on this Quest and without whom none of this would have happened.

Lightning Source UK Ltd.
Milton Keynes UK
UKHW021420130919
349680UK00002B/4/P